Black American Entrepreneur in China

Connecting Industry and Cultural Differences

Black American Entrepreneur in China

Connecting Industry and Cultural Differences

William D. Frazier

Shanghai-America Direct Import & Export Co. Ltd.
Publisher

Black American Entrepreneur in China

Connecting Industry and Cultural Differences

ISBN (978-1-7349182-0-5)

FIRST EDITION, April 2020

Printed in the United States of America by William D. Frazier
and Shanghai-America Direct Import & Export Co., Ltd
(https://xmftrade.com)
Instagram: william_d_frazier
Email: frazierdw@xmftrade.com

Editor: Shuan Von Blerk; Cover Design by Peng Rui

DEDICATION

This book is a foremost dedication to the foreseeable economic transition of international business agreements for Black American small and medium sized enterprises (SME) in the global economy. The vision for this book is to provide a blueprint for black America entrepreneurs to achieve a diversified and sustainable economic growth through business development with the greater China region. These entrepreneurs will acquire access to several Chinese private industries, which allow them to plan for quality business development and growth opportunities. Their access to international trade is a business necessity with diverse and sustainable foreign partners, which is economically sound, market-driven. It will support and provide jobs with equitable wages, as well as quality products and services to help Black American community life.

PREFACE

This book exists because to be a Black American small and medium sized enterprise (SME) business owner and lack direct access to the worldwide economy is not a trade barrier in itself. The situation merely suggests an entrepreneur will seek alternative approaches on how to benefit from the global economy. I believe Black America SME collective representation with the Chinese private industry is null and void, given global trade does not appear accessible to some entrepreneurs. Their potential   business relationship with China can develop its supply chain network, which will offer breaks in global trade. I perceive some SMEs cannot understand how a foreign trade office can present different international commerce prospects and increase business opportunities. As well as, I notice how other ethnic groups have private global trade offices in the greater China region for their business interests. These companies and individuals come from different countries such as Afcham for Africans, AustCham for Austrians, Colombian-Chinese Chamber of Commerce for Columbians, Danish Chamber of Commerce Shanghai for Danish, European Chamber for Europeans and CCI France Chine for French. Also, the German Chamber of Commerce in China for Germans, InaCham for Indonesian, Irish Chamber of Commerce China for Irish, IsCham for Israeli, China-Italy Chamber of Commerce for Italians and The Japanese Chamber of Commerce in China for Japanese.

Furthermore, MayCham China for Malaysians, MexCham for Mexicans, China-Philippines Chamber of Commerce for Pilipino, SingCham for Singaporeans, and Korea Chamber of Commerce in China for South Koreans. And finally, the Swedish

Chamber of Commerce in China for Swedish, SwissCham Shanghai for Swiss, British Chamber of Commerce in China for Brits, and AmCham Shanghai for Americans. I believe the common purpose of these organizations is to share knowledge, develop business relationships, and gain representation based on race and ethnicity.

- William D. Frazier
方伟利
April 16, 2020

INTRODUCTION

For some Black American small and medium sized enterprises (SME) to a great extent, they do not formulate collective international trade agreements because they focus on contracts through local governmental agencies. As well as transactions through a local licensed industry like a food processing plant, at the same time, they lack direct access to foreign trade offices to promote their products and services to the global market. The lack of access could be because black business organizations, media, churches, banks, entertainers, sports icons, fraternities, and sororities, political members, and pundits don't collaborate to establish foreign trade offices for black America businesses. This book outlines my personal, academic, and professional experiences as to why I believe it's essential to develop international trade offices to focus on Black America's global business interests. The trade office can educate, capitalize, and generate trade agreements to benefit black entrepreneurs within America and abroad.

I understand some entrepreneurs receive information from prominent resources to bid on federal, state, and local contracts as a means to grow their business. The procurement opportunity is not a bad idea; I suspect these same resources do not inform black business owners on how to do business with the greater China region. It is if they have the experience to provide practical projects to enhance direct access to the overseas sector. As well as provide resources so Black American SMEs will improve their international position through trade agreements. I understand a particular focus requires an illustration on how to coordinate business opportunities for them on a global scale.

XI

There are too many conspicuous and influential black people whose focus sometimes is to promote their products to the black community. For some, their business growth is not unusual because they tend to find ways to keep their brand relevant to black consumers. I think their business growth ought to encourage others to focus on how they can manufacture and source their products. In essence, by their influence on specific individuals, interest in their product development can do more good than harm for the black entrepreneur. These individuals promote their products onto black consumers under the presumption to buy from them will imply it's a Buy Black campaign. Without any acknowledgment, others reduce trade barriers, so entrepreneurs will explore how they can benefit from the large-scale market. It is my experience these same influencers, and their brands are unaware of the necessity to support specific foreign trade organizations. Such an overseas trade office will take on the role to connect the difference between Chinese private industries and Black American entrepreneurs to facilitate bilateral trade and arrange events.

In the context, to impose unintentional trade barriers can baffle the black business community because many states have foreign trade offices in such countries as Africa, Asia, Australia, Europe, the Middle East, and the Americas. I think within each of these international trade offices, which operate with professional people ready to help multi-national businesses expand into those particular markets. These offices do not have a sizable number of Black American staff members whose primary function is to represent black American SMEs' interests on a global scale. In the short-term, a sizable staff will include black

XII

logistics personnel, black educators, black economic advisors, black interns, and black study abroad participants. Without a sizable black American workforce to represent SMEs' business interest from foreign countries such as China, an SME must understand and acknowledge they will continue to be at an economic disadvantage on a global scale. There isn't a Black American foreign trade office in China, which happens to the world's second-leading economy - and soon to be leading - remains a mystery. It further remains a mystery because, in America, there are collaborative opportunities of various forms among the black chamber of commerce, urban leagues, trade associations, political leaders, and business leaders. I trust a foreign trade office in China will focus on a Black America economic plan, and give SMEs the perception they are serious about the significance of global growth. With the distraction, we tend not to connect our expertise to different business opportunities within the greater China region. The U.S. media-driven society inundates black culture through fashion, sports, entertainment, and celebrity lifestyle issues. To me, it is undeniable Black America has a culture and economic impact on America. The black influence is ingrained into every component of America's life to include music, sports, entertainment, and the celebrity lifestyle. But the Black American SME has not transformed into substantial economic growth for the black community.

If the transformation is not valid, then some black entrepreneurs, HBCU students, and business owners can start to engage in practical proficiency to access the global market. When an attempt to do so, they will expect others to push back; not because to access the worldwide market means they have access to different resources. It merely means they have developed the capacity to create a supply chain network to focus on Black America's global business growth. So from the business opportunity viewpoint, I sense once we access the overall market, economic justice, and income inequality might become an afterthought for black individuals. Also, those who push back against our access, their concern will be to control what pertinent information is necessary to access the global market. I foresee the black over-class can be solution providers for SMEs within the process because their primary financial resource and infrastructure support does require the establishment of a foreign trade office in China. I have confidence in their unique position within the political, business, and education community can be of great benefit to black Americans SMEs' access to the global market.

Some black over-class receives performance-based income has either been political officials, employees, or retirees from senior-level positions in corporations, governmental agencies, military institutions, academia, business arena, entertainers, and sports figures. I concede some individuals will become cautious when there's talk of a foreign trade office in China. An overseas office to promotes economic values, culture exchange, shared history, job creation, and business development through Mainland China for Black America will become problematic. Black American SME should not allow doubts, and racist policies deny them to have direct access to the Chinese manufacture and product source providers. Primarily when the U.S. allocates almost one hundred percent of all of its possessions to include property, capital, influence, resource, advantages, and entitlements to control all levels of the government into the hands of the foremost white society.

I believe one solution for an established office is for prominent and influential individuals who are not scared to push back against doubts and racists policies. The push back will be essential to support the establishment of a foreign trade office in China. The office will focus on ways to rebuild communities through black businesses via the global marketplace. Through the process of engagement in international trade with collaborative partners, a substantial percentage of black income will stay confined in target neighborhoods. I empathize with people who live off of two percent of their salaries because they spend sums of their money in stores and businesses, which don't support the black community. In the situation, a change must occur, and it starts with an acknowledgment of how severe a lack of access to the global market is an economic problem for the black American business community.

I conduct a simple exercise for myself, as an optimist, with a sincere interest in Black small and medium sized enterprises. I search for African American foreign trade office, Black American international trade office, or any combination of words from the search engine to find out if such office exists. I then did the same for other ethnic groups and see if they had such offices. I am curious to know if I will uncover any foreign trade office with an exclusive focus on black American business access to the global market outside the United States. I sense if I didn't locate any international trade offices to focus exclusively on Black America business interests, then the absence is a critical opportunity for a transformation into action. We need to establish our own foreign representative trade offices to support the most and delivery resources to black American businesses so they can rewrite the current structural economic inequality.

The focus will be more on Black America's global economic interest via global manufactures in consumer electronics and appliances, apparel, accessories, and consumer goods, automobile high-end intelligent equipment, food and agricultural products, medical equipment, and medical care products and trade in services rather than other nonessential interest. We must scrutinize domestic entities and create international agreements so black people can have access to international commerce opportunities at the forefront of the global economy. We can start to rebuild our communities and build businesses to support our core values, culture, history, and job creation. Black institutions such as media, churches, entertainment, education, sports icons, or political members can transform the black community with their resources to support black American businesses' access to the global marketplace.

I realize there is no legitimate foreign trade organization in The People's Republic of China with the sole purpose of the development of Black America's SME partnership with Chinese private industries. Its absence is unfortunate since it can be the catalyst to promote black American products and services within the greater China region and beyond. With the lack, an alternative foreign trade office will never create these organizations' international development strategies. For me, the idea to connect the difference between Black American SMEs with Chinese private industries requires an enormous amount of practical knowhow encompasses a fundamental visionary approach. An approach will propel significant advantages such as the ability to take a leap of faith, overcome social obstacles, embrace the foreign culture, change dietary habits, and understand foreign idioms. The specific purpose documents how to develop trade agreements with Chinese private industries and an adaptation into the Chinese lifestyle.

A purpose derives from experiences to intertwine my academic, professional, and individual adaptation to advocate for Black American SME engagement within The People's Republic of China. With more than thirty combined years as a fixed-price supplier, a revenue-generation contract specialist for quality-of-life organizations, spare part specialists for a quasi-government facility, and an administrator of construction, commodity, and service contracts for a local municipality. The book depicts exposure to personal business development occurrences as an adolescent from pubic housing who later became a procurement specialist, economic development planner, urban studies graduate, and study abroad participant. It is not until I became and a co-founder and global business developer of a Mainland Chinese private company to import and export manufacture and source commerce ready merchandise for foreign and domestic clients, I understood the need to improve black America's access to the greater China region.

TABLE OF CONTENTS

Get More Done In Less Time

I grew up in a 1960-70s Brunswick, Georgia public housing community and because of this environment, as an adolescent and youth, I observe my mother's technique on how to "get more done in less time." My guess is the technique helps her to focus on our family well being with minimal economic resources in a low to moderate-income neighborhood. The implementation of her freeze cup business reveals how she acquired additional income with a niche product and creates a supply chain network for the development of her business. Within her business model, she handles operational issues such as risk management, sustainable development, and social and community responsibility. All of these areas are essential to strengthen and promote business growth. Her years as an entrepreneur starts with different color freeze cups to sell in our low-moderate income neighborhood. The idea is to provide a dynamic product concept soon spread throughout the area. The freeze cup is a particular product to cool your body in the summer heat. It is a frozen blend of single color favor water in an eight-ounce paper cup. Some of her product colors are red, grape, and lemon, orange, pink, lime, and blueberry, favor freeze cups. I witness the emotion and wishes radiated by an infinite number of customers with a particular color preference. Before the time, I never recognize her supply chain system to sustain the specific item, which offers a different taste for individual clients.

To continue the sustainable operation, she develops a supply chain system, which includes the local purchase of eight-ounce paper cups, crystal sugar, Kool-Aid mix flavor variety packages, and a deep freezer for production. Her supply chain system has a determinant influence – positive or negative – on other family members and me. When she launches a new product line, a simple request to go to the grocery store to purchase those items has the power to trigger an immediate response. We all understand a harsh reaction, material crises, and damage control to her business reputations are of utmost importance. Her supply chain system became a particularly useful process to maintain her brand's image and reputation as a strategic neighborhood business owner. Even though some favors are necessary for a long-term commitment, others were quite difficult to promote with her customers. Those freeze cups are a product to get additional funds to encourage the family commercial and financial activities. I imagine she knows the product will require more creativity when it comes to her customer base. And for me, I knew I needed more experience to understand my role and to continue her entrepreneurial influence. In a sense, I sought to be supportive of her business venture, be proactive, and create more business transactions – and not wait for them – which is crucial to our family business success. I also notice how other businesses such as barbershops, BBQ pit, and café taught me about the potential economic impact has on success and failure in our local community. The longer we wait to participate, the harder it becomes to present our economic, social, and political clout to the worldwide market.

My mother's ability to get more done in less time opens up opportunities to do business with freeze cups. I will never have thought possible. The development of her freeze cup is because a rapid shift in economic conditions allows the merchandise to be competitive. More often than not, she chose to win dominance in local markets and overcome supply chain barriers in such markets. The context of economic equity demonstrates the extent to which she made a decisive difference. Her merchandise is capable of reducing competition between supply chain and customer base; the latter is the primary means to supply chain. I believe the freeze cup example restores the basic need for small and medium sized enterprise (SME) business is a simple path chosen for cost-effective growth.

In 2000 thru 2001, as a graduate student in Urban Studies at Savannah State University (SSU), an economic development planner for the City of Savannah and part of a team to revitalize specific commercial corridors to support SME development. It is our mission to design a revitalization plan for the commercial corridors within the Community Development Block Grant (CDBG) area or the "CDBG Target Areas Commercial Corridors." Commercial corridors are geographic concentrations of interconnected businesses and institutions, specialized suppliers, service providers to compete and cooperate. What became evident to the team about the mission is the challenge to foster employment opportunities beyond the tourism industry's low-pay service sector jobs. To create ancillary business development expands the purchaser's power and financial stability of low-moderate income residents. I recognize through increase black entrepreneur activities, new business startups, and commercial revitalization; there is a potential for SME within target areas to share in the local generation of wealth by specific industries. When outside ethnic groups sell their product and services into target areas, they tend not to give back in forms of investment and job creation to the region. It's my observation they do not share in the local generation of wealth for the community and less

P

economic equity. There is a need for these target areas to receive information about overseas products and focus on investment and job creation.

Our team every Thursday has a brainstorming session to determine how best to get Black American SME direct access to particular manufacture and source products to sell in their community and bring investment and jobs within their community. I notice two external factors will possibly hinder our ability to prepare these entrepreneurs to be more competitive with other ethnic groups. First, they do not have direct access to Chinese private industries for similar or better products than their competitors. Second, they do not have direct access to a foreign trade office in China to focus on their specific business needs and requirements. I believe when an SME requests assistance to manufacture and source their products in a sense, they do not receive adequate information. The lack of data for these entrepreneurs indicates the control is a necessity to delay direct access. Some information will be outside our office decision-making process and not consider a standardized practice and regulation to provide. The type of resource required will inspire municipal economic development offices to provide the international manufacturer and product source procedures. In particular, information to focus on import and export, customs clearance procedures, and how to have shipments deliver to define locations. I know they need proper procedures for engagement with Chinese private industries to benefit target entrepreneurs.

As a municipal economic development planner, I believe our obligation is to support target communities SMEs' potential business growth even if it involves probable overseas partnerships. As well as provide assistant to promote their product and services to a foreign consumer market. One area for black individuals to start collaboration is with Chinese private industries to obtain landmark projects with mutually beneficial development. I believe any community development organization can initiate mid-level discussions to launch business expansion projects for SMEs with the greater China region. They can take ownership of commercial expansion prospects to demonstrate SMEs' ability to secure international trade agreements with other countries and areas in the world. I sense the more practical experience SMEs receive from municipal economic development offices to create platforms to engage with Chinese private industries, the more appreciative they are within target communities.

My experience of having lived, studied, and commenced with trade business agreements in the Asia Pacific provides me with unique crucial insight. The specific ideas involve adventure, exposures, and all-out breaking down trade barriers forced me to unlearn and relearn certain situations to focus on collaborative opportunities. There were situations were mutual prospects allows me to recognize my Chinese counterparts' assets in specific business industries. I understand there are possible eighteen commercial trades with different requirements to manufacture and product source from the Chinese private sector. Within these various sectors exist collaborative opportunities to acquire information and focus on business growth. I realize for future collaboration; there is a need to appreciate how particular information is pertinent to establish agreements between Chinese private industries and black entrepreneurs. Any potential collaborative agreement can be chosen from specific business industries to include electronic commerce, textile industry, leather & feather, metal product, glass, ceramics, and furniture industry. Also from construction, household appliances, art ware and stationery, sporting, paper-making and printing, machinery manufacturing, petrochemical industry, pharmaceutical industry, food and beverage, motor and bicycle, shipping/vessel, and automobile industry. I have met SMEs who are anxious about their lack of access to the foreign manufacturer and product source providers. They have to deal with competitors in their local market, which only intensifies their situation. The same competition requires most owners with limited time and energy the ability to develop relationships with Chinese private industries. For me, the solution to the problem will not become particularly noticeable when the lack of direct access from SMEs continues from 2002 to present day.

I sense it is essential for the formation of a foreign black trade organization to pursue direct access agreements with Chinese private industries. The pursuit will allow organizations to share the development of an international manufacturer and product source program with Black small and medium sized enterprises. I believe the black small company owners can enhance their global growth prospects while they apply desirable attention to domestic competition. I further realize the lack of foreign expertise is a significant oversight within the black business community. I observe how black social media opinions do not emphasize strategic business relations with the world's second-leading economy. Their outlooks do not come when there is a significant shift in global economic influence. The unrecognizable transformation involves economic growth in developing countries and a decline in economic impact for developed countries. I sense the change in economic importance will continue to disguise information at the black community level, or more precisely, at the notion, Buy Black campaigns are the first commercial solutions to accelerate economic equity. I believe a reasonable offensive will be to overcome a lack of information about Chinese private industries with an underline purpose to marginalize Black businesses from the global economy. It's a necessity direct access to the greater China region becomes a top priority Black American SME global influence strategy.

A strategy I comprehend, at some point, involve a collaborative effort to understand China. I continue to make an effort to engage the people, its commercial development, and how Black America can benefit from it. Or maybe I will devise a strategy to ensure the information will filter down to the black community. I give strategic credence information that is necessary to encourage Black entrepreneurs to develop mutual partnerships with their overseas counterparts. Through such cooperative efforts, they can expand employment with their people and provide quality products to the community. And yet, even though these essential outcomes are critical points for low to moderate communities. It's unfortunate in addition to these outcomes; they are the same conversation points I hear as an adolescent to include affordable homes and health care issues. It is indispensable for the creation of an innovative foreign business program for Black America SMEs to provide direct practical business opportunities with oversea counterparts. A mere suggestion is the program identifies, advances, and protects their interest with the utmost integrity. Even though the proposition may sound simple, it will be problematic for some black entrepreneurs to unlearn and relearn a specific mindset from previous setbacks. Setbacks disallow them to recognize formable prospects to connect the difference because their business influence is necessary but yet obsolete in such countries as China.

For me, it is how to build a bridge to connect the difference between target communities, entrepreneurs, and massive Chinese private industries. So my evolution into the concept commences to manifest itself upon commencement of various leaps of faith actions. The first onset is the participation of the 2000 and 2001 study abroad program to China. Next is the acceptance as an overseas Ph.D. candidate in Shanghai, China, as well as my interest in the part-time foreign English teacher industry. Thenceforth came the break to become a co-founder of a Chinese import and export private company, and next to a decisive leap of faith is to marry Peng Rui from Guiyang, Guizhou Province. Even though these various events occur over twenty years, I commence to acknowledge "connect the difference" concept is a vision given unto me. There are other entities in China on an international capacity to assist foreign and domestic companies and government individuals to operate their own business. And when it comes to the development of individual trade agreements between SMEs and Chinese private industries, I perceive a necessity to advance a definitive cooperative business relationship. I contemplate the absence of a collective representative presence in China; the business perception is an afterthought on how to solicit these industries for SMEs' economic interest.

Small and medium sized enterprises in some target communities need to create, expand, and acquire Chinese counterparts to support their business interests when they don't have a presence in China. For me, the things I do today might signal to others where the possibilities are, where the future lies. Because of today, as in my past experiences in China, I consider our economic future lies in the ability to create new cooperatives through overseas trade offices as a foundation for economic development, wealth creation, and to rebuild and strengthen our community. What I commence to notice is there are some intricate trade barriers I come up against when I attempt to engage in a business relationship in the greater China region. I have to overcome some of those trade barriers involve payment method, quality control, logistical solutions, design concept, custom clearance, and language. In 2004, from the very first challenge, I struggled to manufacture some outdoor flags; I had to understand how raw material entangles other cost components for production purposes. Some of the lack of familiarity involves how manufacture and product suppliers' prices set material grade, product function, and design specifications. I did not know if there were any domestic and export restrictions for particular merchandise. And if so, I need documents, which contain conditions to allow such permission. To me, it is evident to the salesperson I had a deficiency in Chinese cultural skills. My attempt to do trading in the country requires a range of competencies and experience not readily available to me. The skills include areas such as a working expertise of the Chinese language, customs, and culture. I did not have a local partner in the form of a joint venture, which made it impossible for me to acquire the necessary skills to enhance my competitiveness. All I had is an invoice for the payment method. And within the process, I commence understanding once I have direct engagement with Chinese private industries, an instantaneous change from the impossible to the possible became normal circumstances.

I commence to appreciate at any given moment; it takes enormous internal drive and external breaks to form my business mindset about China. And by internal forces, I meant a divine or spiritual insight I cannot comprehend. My ambitions to overcome the lack of business understanding about the flag manufacturer process raise some serious concerns from the salesperson. Other than a payment invoice, I receive instruction to ask for the commercial invoice, packing list, bill of lading, and product description from the factory. Because of the concern, which, as a consequence, provides spontaneous information, allows me to manage the project strategically. Within the process, I commence recognizing external trade opportunities in China revitalize how my combined experience as a procurement officer and economic development planner came to practical use. Combinations where Black American SMEs can look at China's import and export laws and regulations, its geopolitical climate, its population and culture, and its transportation system. And it is the external context Chinese private industry and target businesses can develop product and trade service agreements. In a sense, I learn how to connect the difference between different entities whose previous interactions did not involve direct foreign trade. I know it's one thing to recognize typical stereotypes facilitate through third party media outlets, and still be able to develop an individual business agreement which will benefit both parties. One which involves direct collective face-to-face conversations, so SMEs and the Chinese private business can overcome negative stereotypes to cultivate stronger relationships.

As I commence to focus on business opportunities in China, I became more assertive about which forms of collective trade agreements can set about to grow into fruition. And like with most trade agreements comes due diligence, the one thing requires my protection, if nothing else, is my confidence to see it through. I cannot ill afford to lose my center and opportunity to obtain knowledge about how to discuss trade with Chinese private industries. And within the discussion process, it's an unknown situation as to how much recollection expertise from one sector is transferable into another is more beneficial to community growth and development. Some will argue money follows confidence. Others will claim our diverse leadership style follows a conviction. But seldom will someone disagree entrepreneurship confidence is something we must generate every single day. And as such, I am realistic about how much of the proficiency is transferable to the Black America SME community.

I continue to review which types of trade resources in China are more suitable for me to develop individual opportunities with available Chinese counterparts. I deemed the process is necessary because business engagement with Chinese private industries can awaken prospects of a foreign trade office will be in Shanghai, or maybe not. What has gotten me to the point is with the support of some Chinese counterparts with a confidential global mindset. And I will argue if Black America continues to rely on domestic projects only; and not push for expansion into the global markets, our collective wealth can crash down again. I believe our past, present, and future domestic projects will only take some Black community's economic growth so far. So in 2002, upon my relocation back to Shanghai, China, I discover why most target community's competitors are confident about their business engagement with China.

The discovery is for me to move forward with a business relationship with China; it's easier for me to hold my integrity one hundred percent of the time than ninety-eight percent of the time. The principle is necessary because one lesson I understand as a Black American man in China who advocates for SMEs is the boundary — my moral line — is powerful because I refuse to cross it. I justify my relocation to China once, and there is zero to stop me from explaining it again. At times, I believe I am a unique person to challenge myself to say I will relocate myself to Shanghai, China, and stick it out. It is not as easy as everybody on the outside might think or maybe came here for the first time. And once I overcame the glamour and nightlife and reality took over, I realize I cannot continue those western meals, and I better learn how to budget on local meals per day. In 2002, I reached a point, which requires me to understand an adaptation to the local Chinese lifestyle is crucial.

So as I commence, I conceive a three years mindset, which later I start to apply to others. I set about to put it in the context. I will give myself a three years window because if I can make it beyond my third year in Shanghai, then I will be able to decide if I desire to stay any longer. I believe after my third year, my decision to stay is because of new opportunities, challenges, and adventures. It is not to say Shanghai is an easy adjustment. I have grown to like the country; despite a certain level of rudeness from particular locals. There are some differences in the intimate environment of Shanghai and other mainland provinces. From my earliest 2000 experience, some of Shanghai's citizenry present a very impolite, awkward, and ill-manner atmosphere for a first-tier city in China. Their assumption is if they announce themselves as Shanghainese, the immediately allows them to act and behave impolitely to all others in the town. The sort of behavior permits some to believe they are more significant than other Chinese because the inner city is where they have the majority. I realize there is a reason for a more considerable responsibility to maintain my focus and not allow the perception to seep into my daily life. And to all others within the urbanized area, Shanghainese is by far a more significant majority. With an intelligent and practical city government, a resident has a superiority complex to all other Chinese. My lack of spoken Mandarin and Shanghai dialect made resettlement matters easier because quarrelsome dialogues did improve both individuals' mind and tongue wit and vocabulary. So through the process, in 2002, I have a unique overseas experience because there aren't any foreign mentors in Shanghai to guide me through the process. And within the environment, it's essential to introduce a different narrative about business prospects with Chinese private industries be brought to SMEs' attention. What I realize is the transfer of knowledge is necessary because of the most three standard manufacture and product source mistakes by some Black American small and medium sized enterprises. First, some tend to assume control over the whole manufacture and product source process. Then they will order products before they can understand the import process. Finally, some fail to list out their product function in the original design concept. Within their chosen business model, the potential SME struggle will look at, among other things, China import and export laws, its political climate, and its transportation system.

Another struggle involves whether or not Black Americans sense a need to travel to China for engagement prospects with private industries. In as many attempts to transfer knowledge about their Chinese counterparts, many SMEs do not make efforts to learn because lack of direct access to manufacture and product source providers. I commence to concede; there is no reason for discouragement from the unfamiliar energy. I am instead more eager to explain how foreign trade models will be beneficial for possible business growth. The Black American SMEs buyer program is a collaboration with Chinese trade organization to promote domestic trade shows. The function of a strategic endeavor can support Chinese manufacturers, and product source providers will meet Black American SME delegations in China. I conceive a Black America foreign trade office can encourage companies to participate since some enterprises need access to overseas trade fairs. These fairs will allow them to meet potential partners face-to-face and take a look at their overseas competitors. In part, there ought to be a Black America foreign trade office to select or certify, a group of international trade fairs for special endorsement. With such approval, they can then work with Chinese private show organizers to obtain specialized services for Black American SME exhibitors. These exhibition designs can enhance their market promotion efforts.

Also, from personal experience, I know these exhibitions can help SMEs to set up displays and promotional materials and arrange for them to meet with a potential Chinese manufacturer and product source provider. Also, small business owners who seek partners can participate in a trade mission. A mission will offer opportunities to confer with foreign business, and government representatives may be helpful in their search. For me, a Black America international trade office can arrange a full schedule of appointments in any chosen province in China. These appointments will include matchmaker trade delegations, co-sponsored by the Chinese private industry, and Black America foreign trade office. They will be short, inexpensive overseas visits made for the express purpose of matching Black American SMEs with prospective partners or licensees in one-on-one interviews. Even though I continue to observe how others might benefit from the Chinese private industry, a model requires preparation, technique, and a little faith. And service charge compensation will be for the first-time participants in the program.

I do enjoy the experience and learn to get more done in less time. As I continue to comprehend how to get more done in less time, I recognize most individuals will not have to travel to China or do business the same way. I acknowledge some industries will not benefit from access to Chinese private sectors the same way; I accept some individuals do not have a leap of faith the same way. I realize everyone will not utilize his or her passport in the same way. And the economic connection between SMEs and Chinese private industries isn't seen the same way. I know everybody does not acquire mentorship the same way. I admit some people do not create his or her niche markets in the same way. And in a sense, I will support those SMEs whose blinders come off so they can get more trade agreements done in less time between themselves and the greater China region.

Even though I did not seek an overall consensus from such organizations, I conceive a reduction in the lack of access to the Chinese private industry must occur to affect economic change within the Black community. I believe it's essential to have a foreign trade office in Shanghai, China, for SMEs to engage with their Chinese counterparts outside the United States. The dedicated office can provide a mutual flow of manufactures import and export products and trade in services between Black America and China. Besides, an organization will fill in gaps where the economic development office fails to provide overseas business opportunities to benefit the black community. I fathom a foreign liaison will facilitate those necessary office procedures doable for every business owner who wants access to the global market.

The principle solution for the type of organization manifests itself to a point where I understand the focus must be the limitation of a black economic development plan and the strength of the Chinese model. First, I recognize all successful economic development plans must be continuous-permanent and long drawn out. Second, business participation and political participation are not two different strategies for economic growth but preferably two sides of the same coin. An organization can be about Black economic development interest suggests black students study at a foreign university, work as an intern in an international trade office, or reside in a foreign country after graduation like China. Third, an economic equity plan must be self-reliant; it must create self-sustainable business institutions. In particular, projects for Black American SMEs to recognize the correlations between international business growth, private wealth, and business success. But they lack exposure to Chinese private industries to collaborate on economic equity projects. I think the task can apply to black individuals who have access and resources in the educational, political, social, and economic systems within the United States.

A foreign trade office can function to identify international business development opportunities for well-to-do Black American organizations. The significance of the function is such black Americans in China can contribute to the reversal of social and economic challenges occurrences within America. As a result, the opportunity to participate in a study abroad program will provide HBCU students the incentive to put their college degrees into practical usage in a foreign country. The conscience shift to expose Black America SME from domestic to international commerce is a significant economic conversion. The global transformation is how I understand why some municipal organizations with worldwide access deter social and economic changes for the Black community. Even with the interest of the business as the subject matter, I believe the role of foreign trade office focus on SMEs is not as a vital interest for state and municipal economic development organizations.

The lack of interest in SMEs is because their concerns and issues are seldom part of their overall international business development scheme. It's essential to demonstrate how to explore international trade agreements with China private industries transferable back to Black communities. There is no evidence a global business strategy and the entrepreneurial sector will not emerge within the black community as a result of a foreign office. I believe an office cannot confine its engagement to black capitalism and then create broad diplomatic discussion about mutual interests in business opportunities. It must intertwine local consumer habits and support black businesses' growth initiatives with substantial involvement in foreign trade affairs. While an international trade office stature may rise from local and national to global status, the size of deals it promotes can escalate, from manufacture and source products made in China to the revitalization of inner-city neighborhood commercial corridors. I sense the ability of Black American SMEs to circulate capital within the black community will be an important legacy as a business owner. I imagine these enterprises need global visibility to influence black entrepreneurs in banking, finance, health, construction, education, and consumer goods sectors to benefit the black community. Their business association can grow over time and sustained communities with subsequent opportunities to support black entrepreneurship.

Along with consumer habits, entrepreneurs can develop foreign trade and the global expansion strategy for their business. Although others may not agree, the thought encourages Black businesses' relationship with China; it will at least offer an alternative approach to collapse the current status quo. I understand the lack of access to Chinese private sectors cannot continue to be a self- imposed barrier for some Black-owned businesses. For some SMEs, the breakthrough can uncover inspirational techniques to push through trade barriers to benefit the black community. An office can utilize tangible resources to develop comprehensive business partnerships when others want to enter the global economy. These partnerships with foreign trade organizations can provide pathways for black entrepreneurs to engage with foreign counterparts.

I believe, for the most part, SMEs ought to value his or her past, present, and future business engagement with China.

Even though my mother has faith in her initial business endeavors, the success of others' engagement with the local business community is necessary as well. She displays a desire to inspire others, which came to the point she ignores internal, and external distractions and focus on her business development. Within the process, I set about to understand a win for her is a win for the black community. So I will start to empathize with those who are hesitant about engagement with China. I know the value China can offer to Black America SMEs. I realize once their work, their efforts, and their results are what will win respect and praise from the black community. The irony of the realization is I understand through business engagement with China private industries; there is a consistent target. It is a target with a constant movement, and the moment requires me to claw, scratch, and kick my way through challenges to achieve a certain level of knowledge. And through the process of--constant obstacles, slight holdups, there is a sense of excitement because of these new challenges. These new challenges led me to consider through certain situations; the most probable experiences clarify definite connections because those experiences allow exposure to the global marketplace. My mother's freeze cup business is one of those intangible experiences on how I can get more done in less time to develop a business relationship with Chinese private industries.

2

CHINA STUDY ABROAD

My graduate years at Savannah State University (SSU) allowed me to assess my participation in the 2000 and 2001 China Study Abroad program. I did not know a study abroad experience exposes various cross-cultural activities include education, professional, and personal fields of study. In so much, there is a continual lack of connection between Black America SME and Chinese private industries. Therefore, unbeknownst to me, the study abroad program set in motion a unique situation to visualize an underutilize connection between Black America SME and Chinese private industries. For one thing, the occasion reveals a resourceful urban studies student recognizes how direct engagement with Chinese private sectors will benefit any SME, making it is just as vital for them to obtain the knowhow to enable such an opportunity.

My involvement with the SSU China Study Abroad set in motion the global mindset to understand how Black America SME can do direct business with Chinese private industries. And thereby create jobs and opportunities for the black community. Even though I lack practical experience, at the time, I acquire academic knowledge about urban studies with a concentration in economic development. Through the study abroad program, I sought to take control of my research about economic growth in China as it relates to urban studies. It so happens I did not focus on how to explore international trade agreements with Chinese private industries transferable back to underserved communities. I focus somewhat on black individuals' continued pattern to purchase for others who do not value their community. So the black community's immediate needs are to create, retain, and expand particular industries sustainable for the black community. I recognize I must participate in the study abroad chance to obtain firsthand exposure to China and its economic development structure.

The period of consciousness is where I feel at peace with myself, have a moment of clarity with my thoughts, and allow them to join together to reveal a purpose. At a particular point, the goal is to concentrate, "What economic development insights I have acquired from my experience to have been able to study, work and live in China since 2000?" The original plan isn't to come to China to study, work, or live. First, I came here to do my thesis in Urban Studies. I have no desire to do my research about anything about America because I knew it would not provide me with enough practical experience about a developing country amid tremendous growth. A development period set in motion after entry into the World Trade Organization (WTO) in 2001. And with a Gross Domestic Product (GDP) of 1.2 trillion dollars in 2000, China is the 6th highest among one hundred ninety-five GDP countries.

I believe one of the primary causes behind China's economic rise is its entrench supply chain network of manufacturers from toys to mobile phones for global consumers. And once China acquires international expertise, it became the world's factory and largest trader. I credit the proficiency includes the ability to produce, store, and export goods to increase the opportunity for urban development. In terms of urban studies research, I sought Chinese utilization of existing infrastructures to assist in the growth and revitalization of urban, suburban, rural communities, and their regions. I commence exploring how international trade agreements with China private industries can be transferable back to Black communities. I took the exceptional opportunity and did a program beneficial to me. At least to my best recollection, I have not known anyone within my immediate circle that has study abroad experience. I understand the importance of researching overseas urban studies issues other than the United States can be a potential exploration. I intend the research will not be just another project to meet academic requirements. And with my earlier experience as a procurement officer, China's position as a global manufacture center seems even more like an economic development trendsetter onto the world scene. I didn't realize the procurement challenges Black America SMEs have not only in the national market but the international market as well. The situation is more evident once I became a China Study Abroad participant.

So it just happens my faculty advisor Dr. HONG Zhaohui is a native of Hangzhou, Zhejiang Province. And one day, during September 1999, while on Savannah State University (SSU) campus, I ask Dr. Hong when he will take me to China? And his response is, "One Day." Now keep in mind up to a point, he is the only Chinese person I have ever known other than the local restaurant owners where you can order shrimp fried rice, and of course, LI Shaolong, aka Bruce Lee. My initial introduction to the Chinese culture goes in the exact order; first, it is Bruce Lee movies; next, it is shrimp fried rice, and it continues with a faculty advisor. And from each of these encounters, I acquire additional life lessons about the culture, such as patience, adaptability, and impact. In February 2000, Dr.

Hong offered me a chance to put together four-one day workshops at SSU to introduce the study abroad program. Of course, I did not decline the opportunity because I demonstrate an earlier interest in China. And if we create a successful program work, then I will get my chance to visit China. So my response is, "Okay." Afterward, he requests I design a beautiful flyer and brochure for the China Study Abroad program. The prospectus and brochure have to include information about the program, admissions, cost, application deadlines, and financial aid and scholarship.

Besides, there is more for me to gain as the only Graduate Assistant to participate in the program. Not only am I overjoyed, but also I have the opportunity to work as the photographer for the SSU China delegation throughout the Summer of 2000. I have further requests to assist Dr. Hong with the operation of the study abroad program. If these occasions take place, I have to submit my proposal approved for independent research in China. And I have chosen the MSUS Summer 2000 course MSUS 8855 Population Growth, and Residential Development taught by Dr. Kenneth A. Jordan during the first short summer session. T h e independent study opportunity allows me to submit a paper, An Analysis on the One-Child Family Policy for Population Growth and Residential Development in Beijing, China. So when people asked me how I did get to China, I often replay, "It took a question to get me to China." But the truth is I have an independent study proposal for MSUS 8855 Population Growth and Residential Development to examine the links between population growth and residential development in Beijing, China, during the second short session of Summer 2000. And as a result of May 18, 2000, proposal I receive a China Study Abroad subsidy of two thousand dollars to help defray my participation cost in the Summer 2000 China Study Abroad program. On May 26 at 11:50 am, I meet my five hundred dollars payment obligation to support the study abroad program. The requirement allows me to continue the project with Dr. Hong in the development of SSU Students Conduct Code, Checklist for China Travel, and Student Schedule.

Even though up to a point, the idea of a China visit is a constant work in progress. On June 5, the excitement came more to the forefront because I obtain my Chinese Visa from the Houston Consulate General of the People's Republic of China. It came five days before our 4th Workshop of China Study Abroad Program in Room 110, Payne Hall on SSU campus. The workshop starts with open remarks from Dr. Joseph H. Silver, Sr. Vice President for Academic Affairs and Mr. Tom Hines, then course introduction by Dr. Olufunke Bowen and Dr. Hong. After, Dr. Hong, Professor Bowen, and I present a review of the student conduct of code. And the final workshop areas by Dr. Hong includes a checklist of travel and essential phone numbers, the program schedule, the introduction of Chinese culture and customs, and learn basic Chinese in China.

On June 26, China Eastern and Air China airlines require us to reconfirm our flights at least three days before departure either from the States or from China. The reconfirmation process insists before July 5; everyone utilizes the telephone number on his or her ticket package to verify his or her ticket. My concern about the repeat verification process is because since we're about to embark for a communist country, maybe they consider someone got cold feet. I receive a letter from Dr. Joseph H. Silver, Sr. which states, "You are about to be part of

Savannah State University history as a result of your participation in the China Study Abroad Program. I congratulate you on being selected and being bold enough to take advantage of the great opportunity. Make the most of it represent yourself, your family, and your university well. Study hard, enjoy, and explore new horizons. Take care and peace be with you". And as a result, on July 8, 2000, at 6:05 am, nine SSU students and two faculty members flew from Savannah International Airport to Beijing, China, which became SSU official first inarguable study abroad program to visit the People's Republic of China.

I am on my way to China with eight SSU students and two faculty members, Ms. Vivien Harris-Murphy, Ms. Pamela Daniels, Mr. Ramon Barboa, Mr. Darnell Blackshear, Mr. Zyon D. Smiley, Ms. Alicia Bailey, Ms. Gloria Strachan, Mr. Scott Witt, Dr. HONG Zhaohua and Dr. Olufunke Bowen on Savannah State University's inaugural China Study Abroad program. On July 9 at 5:10 pm, after a 23hrs 55 minutes flight from Savannah International Airport with connections in Atlanta, Georgia, Los Angeles, California, and Seoul, Korea, we arrive in Beijing, China. We reside in the Yudu Hotel near Capital Normal University (CNU) in Beijing. The ideal location allows students to either walk or ride bikes to the university. Furthermore, the unique experience enables each student to reach a level of cultural competency and understand China, which they will not have been able to acquire otherwise. And as an integral component of the program, SSU presidential delegation led by President Dr. Carlton J. Brown and Vice President for Academic Affairs Dr. Joseph H. Silver, Sr. sign agreements with two Chinese universities to promote exchanges between faculty, students and staff research.

The first signature ceremony happens at CNU, and afterward, we travel to Tiananmen Square and Forbidden City with dinner at Lao Sea Tea House & Beijing Opera. We visit The Great Wall, Ming Tombs, and Summer Palace before SSU presidential delegation next day departure for Shanghai. On July 14, I, along with the SSU presidential delegation, flew from Beijing to Shanghai to visit Shanghai Teachers University (STU). And upon our arrival at Pudong Airport, one of the first words I utter as I depart the plane is, "I am going to live here." The sudden utterance of these words is in no way disrespectful to the residence or capital city, Beijing. Still, Shanghai is a magical attraction with an immediate impact on me. Therefore, the sudden utterance did not attribute to our prearranged visits to STU, The Bund, Shanghai Museum, Antique Market, Chinese Acrobats, or Shanghai Old City Children Institute. I do believe on July 16, while in Pudong New Area, the reason behind sudden utterance came into existence.

It came into existence because up until now; I have no decision in which area to focus my Master Thesis research. But I know I did not want to do research about the United States. I appreciate Urban Studies because, before I arrive in China, I complete an earlier course to provide a systematic study of the development, implementation, and evaluation of policies with particular emphasis on their fiscal impacts. I desire to execute research on a country matters in the long term and make a global difference in a practical sense. The coursework is reminiscent of a conversation with Dr. Hong about Analyzed Groundhog Day: Job Shadow for Savannah High School Students. He provides some critical insights from three different academic perspectives. He informs me if I pursue my

Ph.D., I should let my thesis be the framework of my Ph.D. work. And since my earlier paper submission to Dr. Kenneth Jordan, it appears I am on the right track, so I continue this direction. But he cautions me if I did so, I can lose out on time with my family and friends.

I commence taking notice of the collective atmosphere about economic development in China while on a visit to Jinmao Tower in Pudong New District after we visit Shanghai Old City – Children Institute on a beautiful bright sunny day. I embrace the sort of reinforcement the city can be a place to offer a practical experience without any recognizable barriers. It provides me with a dose of liberation. I pause to observe the laborer high upon an outdoor scaffold to perform some outside maintenance on the tower. And as I continue to stare upwards, I probe Dr. Hong, "What happens to him after he finishes the project; after they finish the building?" And his remark is, "Why don't you find out?" And with a simple response, I start to contemplate how I can accomplish the task. I can do my research about migrant workers and their role in the economic development of China. And I commence my quest to understand more about migrant workers in China.

These migrant workers and Black Americans share similar economic challenges within their perspective countries at different periods. The Black Americans travel from the southern to the northern part of the U.S., known as the Great Migration. In China, the emigration is similar for migrant workers' from the countryside to cities after the 1978 Open Door Policy. I understood the resemblances from both groups involve different cultures, political systems, education levels, and social and economic status. The event educates me to investigate further the critical review of urban studies and its future development in China. On July 17, there is another historic signature ceremony between STU and SSU, further cement SSU China Study Abroad Program among these universities. After the services, President Dr. Carlton J. Brown and Vice President for Academic Affairs Dr. Joseph H. Silver, Sr. proceed back to the U.S.

Then Dr. Hong and I depart for Beijing to join Professor Bowen and the other eight SSU students just in time to observe the China court system. While the observation is unheard of tourists to witness, a well-known law professor Dr. Zhao Huiman at CNU, arranges the visit. In the courtroom, an officer receives paperwork from the clerk and then proceeds to bring in the male defendant. The defendant is on trial because he sells maps to make money without a permit. The Chief Judge speaks first, and while he stands up, the defendant is allowed to respond to the Chief Judge. Then the prosecutor speaks next; then, the Chief Judge speaks, and then the defendant and police officers sit down. Next, the accuse claimant speaks, and then the defendant replies. Meanwhile, the Chief Judge controls the conversation with the defendant as the clerk records the information into a computerized system. The prosecutor then converses with the defendant, while two police officers change places with new ones. Why? The next sequence of events continues as the Chief Judge speaks to the defendant; the prosecutor speaks to the defendant, and then the advocate speaks to the defendant. Then the Chief Judge speaks to the accuse claimant and defendant. Afterward, the prosecutor talks to the defendant. Chief Judge tells the accuse claimant. Prosecutor speaks. The Chief Judge responds to the defendant. Chief Judge talks to the advocate. The prosecutor discusses with the Chief Judge. The Chief Judge speaks to the defendant and accuses the claimant. The prosecutor explains with the Chief Judge. And then the police bring in the first witness.

The Chief Judge speaks to the witness. The witness signs a document than sits down while the police officer stands up. The prosecutor speaks to the witness, and then the police officer sits down. The Chief Judge speaks to the defendant and witnesses. And then the police officers change to new ones. The Chief Judge talks to the witness while the clerk records the information into the computerized system. The police officer retrieves a document from the clerk for the witness to sign, and then the police officer escorts the witness from the courtroom. Next, the prosecutor communicates with the Chief Judge; and then the Chief Judge speaks to the defendant and prosecutor. The accuse claimant talks to the Chief Judge about the potential damages. The police officer takes a document to the advocate from the accuse claimant. The advocate speaks to the Chief Judge, and then the accuse claimant talks to the Chief Judge and visa versa. The police officer takes the document to the Chief Judge and then sits down. The prosecutor speaks to the Chief Judge. The Chief Judge speaks to the defendant. The advocate speaks. The police officers again change to new ones at 10:27 am. The accuse responds; the Chief Judge speaks to the prosecutor, and then the prosecutor responds. And at the point, the defendant receives a fine and one-year prison sentence. He protests the penalty because he didn't have any money, so he sold maps to make a living in the first place.

In the following days from July 22-August 5, eight students are in class Monday through Thursday in four-hour sessions. The courses are at CNU Central Classroom Building or the Yudu Hotel. At both locations, each student has partnered with a Chinese student at CNU as his or her language partner. They exchange information about American and Chinese Studies and discuss thoughts on US-China relations. They also dined together and became friends. Some of their class-related activities include visits to the Great Wall, Ming Tombs, Tiananmen Square, and the Forbidden City. Besides, they visit a Chinese Senior Home and farm is we exchange songs with the residence.

It is a great honor to visit a Chinese family home. We visit the home of our China Normal University host XI Qingyong where we learn how to make traditional Chinese dumplings. Also, we had a field trip to Tianjin, China, and enjoy a Chinese acrobatic show before our farewell party. Not only did we travel to these various locations to experience China first hand. We participate in activities to further introduce each of us to the Chinese culture. The trip marks the first student initiative for Savannah State University. It is the first program of its kind at SSU in the greater Savannah area and the first Historically Black College or University (HBCU) in Georgia to establish a study abroad agreement with institutions of higher learning in China.

For me to participate in the China Study Abroad Program at the particular time is a life-alter experience. I have the opportunity to develop a new perspective on almost everything as it relates to Black Americans' participation in procurement, supply chain management, economic development, and urban studies within a communist country. My mind has taken me to areas where most individuals cannot visualize the procedures on how to develop economic development projects with a foreign country. In 2000, the interaction with Chinese people had put me in awe because my conceptual makeover went from excitement to intellectual curiosity, to their economic development transformation in such a short period. The unique experience behind the conceptual makeover is a combination of an intensive independent study project, firsthand observation of Chinese society through frequent field trips, guest lectures, and trips in Beijing, Shanghai, and Tianjin. Also, the unique experience challenges me to reach for a higher level of cultural competency to understand China will be useful in the globalized world.

And to demonstrate the higher level of imaginative skill, SSU, and Chinese Benevolent Association and Chinese Professional Club in Savannah is eager to hear the presentation and report about China upon our stateside return. For the most part, the event is a challenge because the display is to the Chinese community. I have to propose something to the group already knows everything about China. Therefore, my involvement is about the most memorable event, person, and sightseeing I witness in China. And, of course, is the day I saw a migrant worker high on a scaffold outside the Jinmao Tower. It is the day; I determine to do my Master Thesis research about the role migrant workers have on the economic development of China. On September 3, 2000, I gave a presentation about the difference between Chinese and American cities at the Chinese Benevolent Association located on Howard Floss Drive Savannah, Georgia.

So, in a lull of the event, I commence reflecting upon the occurrence with a little more appreciation about China and Chinese people. The gratitude did not just last minute or so, but it provides me with more clarity about what it meant to be an economic development planner. It is within the time of clarity, where I can understand why SMEs need assistance to engage in foreign markets. I recognize the effects globalization will have on SMEs. I can differentiate between one-system talks about SME development but has barriers to deter particular groups. Yet another method does not talk about SME development but has policies, benefit entrepreneurs. And at the point, I develop more interest in the revitalization of inner-city neighborhood commercial corridors. I have more awareness because the initial China experience demonstrates how economic development can be transposed from an academic to a practical proficiency within a blink of an eye.

As a matter of fact, with the newfound consciousness, I commence understanding the difference between each countries entrepreneurial efforts and lifestyle pleasures. The Chinese did not talk about opportunities to create business for others; they do business to create those opportunities. Whereas the U.S. talks about opportunities to creates business for others, but they create barriers to prevent those opportunities. When SSU asked me to lead another study abroad group back to Shanghai in July 2001, I cannot say yes fast enough. And while on the particular study abroad trip, I plan to attend the World Planning Congress held at Tongji University in Shanghai.

3

Leap Of Faith

Founded in 1907, Tongji University, a non-profit public higher education institution located in Shanghai, offers courses and programs to lead to bachelor, master, and doctorate degrees in several areas of study. It has a selective admission policy where international students are welcome to apply for enrollment. In March 2001, it merged the Architectural Design and Research Institute of Tongji University and Shanghai-Tongji Planning and Architect Design and Research Institute. The union forms the new Civil Engineering and Architect and Design Institute of Tongji University. The institute rank in the General Appraisal of Shanghai Exploration and Design Units of Tongji University rose from the sixth position in 2000 to the fifth position in 2001, and third in 2002. In early November 2001, I decided to seek enrollment in Tongji University's Spring 2002 Urban Planning Ph.D. program after receipt of an acceptance letter from the university. When I made the decision, it reminds me of a previous statement upon my arrival in Shanghai.

The significant difference between the Summer 2000 study abroad and Spring 2002 Ph.D. program is the study abroad has a one-time single entry thirty-day visa expiration date, which meant no matter what, I had to leave China within thirty days upon entrance. Whereas the Ph.D. program stipulates, I have sufficient capital to support my overseas educational endeavors. And to accumulate those necessary funds, I start to sell personal possessions, and what I will not sell, I either gave away or donate to charity. When family, friends, and employer commences asking if I am going to move to China. Are you ready to leave the U.S. and live in a communist country where you know no one and no one knows you? And I said yes, I am going to move to Shanghai in February 2002 to attend Tongji University. I feel comfortable with the decision. I have no problem with the relocation process because of my previous experiences as a study abroad participant. I accept the personal challenge and look forward to a leap of faith because it's the right move for me.

Upon my arrival in Shanghai, I had no immediate job to provide a continuous flow of income. For individuals like me who did not work for any company, an English teacher job offers some revenue. Even as a suitable short-term, part-time job, I knew the situation would not be a long-term means to make a decent income. As an English teacher, it allows me to become more familiar with Chinese culture. I will get more done with less time when I transform some classroom events to work more to my advantage. I taught classroom communication forums in English to middle school students, college students, and adults in the academic and private sectors for about a year or so. Our classroom discussion involves issues for them to understand more about Black America. While at the same time, I realize from their perspectives what they believe life can be like for a Black person in China. I understand from each classroom forum on how to study, live, and work and dos and don'ts in China.

For example, pork is available but not eaten by me; they suggest at the dinner to sample every dish possible. The sample food is positioned communal in the center of the dining table, and everyone helps himself or herself. It is both polite and encourage to and remarking aloud with 'eating noises' you enjoy the food. They suggest I have several alcohol toasts with the phrase 'gan bei.' Since I did not drink alcohol, I will toast with tea or hot water. One of the most critical pieces of advice I acquire from them is how to do business with China. They inform me if I want to do business in China, I will learn from Wenzhou people. They believe people from Wenzhou, Zhejiang Province know how to create endless business opportunities.

In early 2002, there are several aspects I had to understand about China other then there were a lot of people here with different features, personalities, wants and needs, and mannerisms. It is a vast market not to offer any mentorship; I had to find my unique niche and learn how to eat, clothe, and house myself. I had to create a significant role, allows me to utilize my education and work experience, which is sought-after in Shanghai. I know the position will be beneficial; it still requires some black entrepreneurs or any Black American organization in the States needs it as well. I knew back in Savannah, there were black-owned businesses desire direct access to China, but they didn't possess the knowhow to do so. But for me to get to a point, I had to learn more about China. As I continue to proceed in the direction, I contacted such organizations in Shanghai, such as the Georgia Department of Economic Development and Shanghai American Chamber of Commerce to obtain business opportunities. But the same business obstacles exist in the states commence to revere itself in Shanghai. To support Black American SMEs with the exchange of knowledge to access the more significant Chinese consumer is not their focus.

While in China, knowing the probable response continues to excite me about the possibilities to make a difference. The unconceivable perception about these prospects is I start to appreciate why I came here. I did not know anything about China before my study abroad experience. There is a limited amount of information about China from local news outlets in southeast Georgia communities. But as an international student and English teacher, I commence to recognize SMEs' lack of direct access to business opportunities in China. Since I am not in America, six experiences made better-quality life adjustments in Shanghai. The first is to communicate with family and friends outside China with the usage of a phone card to permits stateside calls. Another change is to the food in China. I did not know pork, which I do not eat is the most popular meat. The third is there are lots of spicy foods I cannot handle. Tasty food like Sichuan dishes makes me sneeze and cough without any control. There are few foreign grocery outlets in Shanghai, except for Carrefour-French and Metro-Germany grocery outlets. By comparison, several item prices are higher than local merchants. I am not sure if the food quality from the neighborhood market is up-to-par due to what appears to be inappropriate sanitary conditions. At the point, I can be biased because of my previous experience with different overseas grocery outlets in Shanghai. I made the fourth adjustment and learned how to purchase groceries from the local farmer markets. As a result, I start to prepare my daily meals with produce from the neighborhood market.

I commence purchasing various meats, fishes, green vegetables, dried beans, small celery, thin skin green peppers, potatoes, sliced eggplants, cabbage, eggs, and a bag of snow vegetables from local merchants. But then I realize when hungry, nothing can compare to a bowl of soup and Lanzhou Chaofan.

i.e., fried rice with bits of mixed vegetables, beef, and fried eggs. Although the dish is inexpensive, it fills me up and is available throughout the country. I always know what to order since I seldom know what I'll get when it comes to street food. I'll educate others last-minute late-night meals have to wait until morning because dietary changes can cause a physical reaction at the most inappropriate time. The final two adjustments are the most difficult for some locals to handle. I do not drink alcohol in any form, nor do I smoke. From the time when I need to develop relationships in China, my counterparts understand these two issues are not part of the process. But continues to excite me about the possibilities to make a difference; these six changes are easy to maintain.

I inform others it's easy to acclimate themselves to China. For me, the natural part is I witness some of Shanghai's economic processes do not exist in southern Georgia. In 2001, Jinmao Tower had the tallest hotel in the world and was the tallest building in Shanghai. There are four metro lines in Shanghai, i.e., Line 1 (North to South), Line 2 (East to West), Line 3 (Inner ring), and Line 4 (Outer ring). I can learn more about the city because of these metro lines. As a result, I commence to witness the growth of the town, and I sought to engage more in that growth. After China's 2001 admission into the World Trade Organization (WTO), I found a way to understand the growth of the city. As a study abroad participant, it is a natural process to utilize most of these metros lines in my daily activities as necessary. In 2002, the metro system was not the primary transportation mode for my life in Shanghai. I soon discover the public bus system is not a big issue when I explore the more dense populous neighborhoods. For me, these public bus routes provide tours throughout Shanghai dense urban growth and development communities. These municipal transports are very cost efficient, and I cannot experience Shanghai without them and the metro lines. Whereas, I sense I can do without taxis as much as possible.

I set about to recognize the public bus system challenge my sense of direction just a little more than the metro lines because of multiple bus stops and location per stops. The metro stop signs have pinyin and Chinese characters on the upper inside train cabin walls, whereas public bus signs are only displayed Chinese characters on the top inside bus walls. I understand it's a challenge to recognize which bus stop I need to get off. To get a better feel for the city and improve my recognition of Chinese characters, I often ride the bus from the original point of departure to the last stop. And once I can understand the route, I will depart the bus somewhere in the middle where I can explore a particular neighborhood. It became less of a challenge to engage in the local community as time past because I go about to become somewhat mindful of the lifestyle in Shanghai. The routine doesn't bother me as much as it might others who either arrive here for a study abroad program or as a tourist.

One of the most noticeable local behaviors will sometimes bother me is what I will call, "Stop and Stare," which is okay by all standards. It is okay because I can proceed to my final designation without any potential life threatens incident. Unlike Stop and Frisk, I can end up dead or in jail as a black person in the States. I am from the southern part of the U.S., and one thing I will sometimes encounter is some people will stare at me for unknown reasons. And the stare happens in a common area like a shopping mall. So when somebody in the South looks at me, my usual reaction will be to speak to let him or her know I see him or her. And of course, they will follow up with a simple hello. But in Shanghai, when I said hello after eye contact, most people do not respond. So I said, "My goodness, this is rude." I spoke, but he or she did not talk back. I will wave, but he or she did not wave back. Then I ask myself, "Why do they look at me with such a deep stare"? So little did I know, in most cases, I can be the first black person they had ever seen. And for me, the interaction has to be one of the most significant mindset adjustments as I explore the city. If I am stateside, my thoughts will have been to prepare for an unpleasant incident. But in actuality, the likelihood of the sort of interaction in Shanghai is very rare. I am like, "Okay, there will not be any incident here, and I am cool with their stares, and if I am quick on my feet since they want to take pictures together, I will charge 10RMB for ladies; 20RMB for men; and children are free." And from the commerce opportunity, I can raise enough money to pay for my daily meals in Shanghai, maybe.

So every day, as I prepare to work and study in China, I make an important decision. And the choice is, how do I go about to build a beneficial connection between Black America and China? How do I stay committed to the decision? I made a promise to myself, and to the universe, I am serious about the connection. I contribute a positive narrative about Black America to the Chinese culture. And even if I fail along the way, I am firm and resolute with the process. But for it to be a correct decision, I must possess the self-discipline to see it through to the end. And to see it through, I wake up with the purpose every single day while in the greater China region. When I commence and conclude my daily interaction with Chinese people, I continue to connect the difference between Black America and China based on my commitment to do so.

What most people might not have known about me is I sometimes with my foldup bicycle get on a train and travel to other cities near Shanghai. I will travel to other cities like Hangzhou, Ningbo, and Suzhou, to have a healthier China experience. I like to ride my bike in Shanghai, it sometimes became tiresome, and I am ready for the adventure. I enjoy the type of outdoor adventure because it offers a way for me to focus on a task for a few hours without external distractions. When I spend time in other less densely populated cities, my body functions with less strain because there's plenty of space. And when I ride my bike, the exercise improves my blood pressure, digestion and provides my immune system an extra boost. I cannot forget other benefits, such as a chance to eat other local dishes, visit historical sites, or ride to help keeps my heart and lungs healthy.

Bike rides enable me to fall fast asleep after a day full of outdoor activities. I disconnect with a bike ride for a few hours from others, and I enjoy the natural environment I crave in southeast Georgia. I need the natural environment in outer cities as a reminder to enjoy my China experience. Some of my bikes rides in Hangzhou, Ningbo, and Suzhou occur because of less develop an active outdoor strategy for Shanghai does not include natural environments to maintain my healthy lifestyle. I commence discovering new locations to boost my get-up-and-go so I can enjoy my Shanghai lifestyle. The lack of these natural environments in Shanghai is not to say the city does not offer a healthy lifestyle. It is just Shanghai provides a different flow sparks my other health interest beyond these traditional outdoor activities from one Chinese city to another. Shanghai nightlife is a better option for me in comparison to those other outer cities because one Shanghai nightclub supersedes all the others combines.

Let's sometimes say the way to enjoy the Shanghai nightlife requires engagement in cross-culture exchange of ideas. I sought to experience live old school funk music I travel down to Bourbon Street on Hengshan Lu. From another perspective, when I desire to enjoy new school Rap Music, I journey down to Pegasus on Huaihaizhong Lu. I am fortunate enough to attend a live jazz performance at the Storm of Shanghai (SOS) Club inside Meiluocheng by two homeboys, Phil Morrison Trio featuring Keith Williams. The SOS Club is where Phil and Keith take their inspirational jazz and funk roots to another level on any night. Ah, their music selection propels others to join in and can never be replicated in Shanghai going forward.

Along with Phil manipulation of those incredible bass lines and Keith's magical fingers on those keys, I just know whatever they did, "Just Make it Jazzy and Funky." And that is what they do with such pure music comes from the depth of their souls. SOS Club is no longer in Shanghai; these two brothers took me back to the Marshes of Glynn with their soulful sound. And since there are numerous nightlife activities, I cannot think about how to develop strategic partnerships with Chinese manufacturers and suppliers. My immediate focus is to exchange some traditional cultural awareness with my students so they can gain a better rapport with Black America. The outdoor lifestyle and nightlife offer differentexperiences to allow me to intermingle with Chinese culture.

One of these early 2002 intermingles my friendship with a female migrate worker and her Jianbing breakfast specialty. Our interaction ensues at the construction site of Shanghai South Railway Station location site on South of Huming Road, North of Shilong Road, East of the will-be Guilin Road and West of Liuzhou Road. I became aware the location is the landmark of the world's first-round railway station bears the message "Keeping Pace with the Time." As I travel through the construction site on my way to Tongji University or my residence near Guilin Road, I know one day, the railway station will serve as an interchange of many transportation means. Since my apartment is near Guilin Road, I will often walk-pass her pop up breakfast stand on my way into the city. It just so happens I did not know what's a Jianbing because I made my breakfast due to my stateside lifestyle. I know my student-teacher lifestyle helps me to develop in such a manner, so if anything happens, I am like, "Okay, this is just a normal day here." These developments help me to accept China is the new knowhow. Up until then, my breakfast lifestyle is pretty comfortable, and there is no need to complain too much. On a particular morning, I acquire a new breakfast situation to change my taste buds. I cannot help but make an inquiry with the female migrate worker about her Jianbing breakfast specialty. Her ingredient did not have adequate covers; there is no need to criticize how she prepares what resembles a burrito. I have to remind myself per my hidden stateside bias about the way things are in China.

Once I bit into Jianbing, I confess to her through my body gesture and facial expression she has another customer. I know she's more appreciative of my efforts to connect our cultural differences via her Jianbing specialty. I treasure these intermingle with everyday Chinese people. I go about to see other migrant workers and farmers with their desserts and snacks made from rice. Some will have Jianbing, sweet potatoes...umm, what else will they have? Oh yeah, I see others with more vegetables over there. I even witness others in what appears to be a portable hot pot over there...yes, hot pot on wheels. It's the type of intermingling to remind me of the local lifestyle here in China. I never thought I'd get the sort of introduction to China. Wow, it looks like these migrant workers and farmers provide an excellent service to the country. And I will have to consider Shanghai has a local lifestyle of migrant workers and farmers with different skillsets. I have no idea my connection with them will be so vital to my self-development in the realm of future educational pursuits in China.

Upon my Fall 2002 admission as a Ph.D. candidate into Tongji University Urban Planning program, the burden to move beyond an English teacher position begins to weigh on me. I know the Ph.D. program allows me to pursue my interest in comprehending more about economic development in China. But until an alternative financial solution presents itself, I have to teach English to support life's necessities. To become accustomed to China, I commence researching economic development articles to have very little to do with the United States. But more with a focus, China will be so vital to the future development of Black America economic development programs. I understand with the newfound awareness, I have chosen China as a possible pathway to experience what I regard as my life purpose.

One of my earlier experiences is migrant workers in China have similarities to Black America and The Great Migration. So when migrant workers from the countryside sought diverse opportunities in Tier One cities, it reminds me of when Black America migrated from the South to the North. I pursue out how I can use these similarities to understand life in China better; and then how to present these outcomes to Black America. I have to focus on my behavior because I know I need to possess or acquire specific patterns of thoughts and values to contribute to my lifestyle pattern. Within the process, my roles and interests with my landowner, local merchants, students, local community, and other foreign teachers will guide my intra-relationships contribute to a sustainable life in Shanghai.

My choice to relocate back to China is not only about Black America's economic development prospects and market factors but also on the intra-relationships between me in the black business development system. Not to mention China has an unknown economic development tradition with Black America. But there are some hidden advantages, which can play an essential role in our economic development process. It appears China's industrial development will increase the number of scientific and technological personnel, improve production facilities, and has a general increase in the level of knowledge of science and technology as well.

When I transition to China, there is an implementation phase to comprehend some straightforward relations between urban-rural individuals, state-owned units, collective-owned units, and private employers. The upfront relation is how I can show my acceptance for the relationship between all parties. There is a need to initiate new friendships necessary with those individuals with positional power. The direct relation will ensure I maintain my position as a friend to China as well as a Black Man. I have to comprehend real fast how China formulate a series of laws and regulations to coordinate the whereabouts of foreigners, and to develop relationships with various local and international agencies. I know my intra-relationships will improve as my contribution to the Chinese society determines which products and services they provide to me within a given period.

Does China offer a suitable option for Black American business development in the United States? The book illustrates a change in my approach from the United States to China is a direct link to my vision for Black America's economic development. In several district or metropolitan regions can become "mixture of a business collaborative." It is to say; other collaborative can emphasize division within them and be thought of as different specialties because the transition between them reflects diverse populations, consumer culture, and ethnic and social organizations. A mixture of segmented business collaborative into various intra-relationship governs my decisions in different sectors such as housing, jobs, schools, and healthcare.

I notice how some Shanghai districts have an excess of in-migration over out-migration as a comparison to others since the realization of new urban development projects. Such projects include residential community, train station, schools, hospital, and substantial transportation system altogether causes slight inconvenience to the local community. In the instance, China's economic development projects commence to provide significant improvements to the local lifestyle. From November 2002 through July 2003, the process and mechanism for these substantial changes become recognizable with the awareness of a new and severe form of atypical pneumonia. Atypical pneumonia known as Severe Acute Respiratory Syndrome (SARS main symptoms is high fever (>38 degrees Celsius, dry cough and shortness breath, or breathing difficulties. I discover the incubation period is short, estimated to range from two through ten days, with three-five days the most common. I am in the Shanghai area; there is travel restriction to Hong Kong and Guangdong Province by recommendation of The World Health Organization (WHO. The organization's concerns, as well as others, are with the speed of international travel creates a risk case can spread fast around the world. When I call home, family members and friends say, "Don't you come back with that SARS," 'you want to be in China, so stay in China with that SARS." I know they mean well, so to avoid transmission, I inform them to prevent my chances of infections, I notice if others wear face masks. And I'll reduce my outside contact, as necessary. I remind them it is through close contact with an infectious person for the infective agent to spread from one person to another. And some examples include people who cough, sneeze, kiss, share food or drinks, or have contact with contaminated toys, tissues, or surfaces. The majority of cases occur in hospital workers who care for SARS patients and close family members of these patients.

The infectious agent offers China a chance to promote good personal hygiene habits. There are flyers and news resources to inform the public to cover their nose and mouth with a tissue when they need to sneeze or cough and wash their hands afterward with liquid soap or alcohol hand rub. They start to clean public surfaces with dilute bleach (one part bleach to forty-nine parts water), which special attention to doorknobs, railings, light switches, remote controls, and other surfaces people touch. Some people start to use serving spoons when eating from communal dishes. Others commence developing a healthy lifestyle with proper diets, regular exercise, and adequate rest. For me, SARS, the health situation isn't a suitable deterrence to return to the United States. The health crisis illustrates a change in public health initiatives for the betterment of China can be a direct link to possible Black America's SME business opportunities.

4

Do For Self

There is an unintentional disconnect between resource allocation and business opportunities not recognizable within the Black American business community. I often hear within the Black community to do for self. I seldom get direct guidance from our business leaders on how to do for self in the global economy. I suppose China's economic growth commences the process provides beneficial monetary transformations to their local lifestyle. Then the black community will be able to take the model and do the same. I imagine when it comes to adjustment with Chinese business decor, I know I have to obtain specific knowhow from my Chinese counterparts to create cost-effective opportunities. I understand one-day, an open eye experience will be the possible way for me to acquire particular expertise through trade with China. The experience will require I travel to other Chinese provinces and foreign countries in the forefront.

I consider the process to acquire new Chinese experiences will be a continual task; it turns out to be evident for me to spend more time in China. My quest to gain additional insight into China is not my primary commitment to relocation to Shanghai. It just so happens the occurrences of September 11, I set about a life-and-death undertaken between an advanced degree opportunity within a communist country and a war campaign for a democratic one. The event had awakened a previous conversation with Professor PAN Haixiao from Tongji University. I set about to ponder since China is on the cusp to change its urban landscape from an agrarian to a socialist-market system; I had an opportunity to pursue an advanced degree in China. Once I had taken up the task to identify, manage, and revitalize inner-city business corridors for a local municipality, then I can submit those results to a public entity. With the possibility to have an effective change, there is no sense to decide which career path to pursue between the two countries.

I inquiry how Black America small business owners can elude domestic wholesalers and go direct to China for their manufacture and source products. The importance of the question occurs more after China's admission into the World Trade Organization (WTO) on December 11, 2001. For me, it ensures a significant wake-up call for a strategic economic development initiative for Black America entrepreneurs who desire direct access to China manufacturing industries. The access exposes these entrepreneurs to products at fair and reasonable prices compete with their domestic wholesalers. It is just as crucial for me to visualize how to develop resources in China to assist black businesswomen, black businessmen, black entrepreneurs, and black startup in benefiting from international markets. Of equal importance, Black America small businesses must engage with Chinese factory owners even when methods for direct access are not an established focus point within the black community.

There will be a need for continuous dialogue to promote Black America's ability to develop direct business ties with Chinese factories. To establish a foreign Black American trade organization to share its expertise and business ideas with the black community. Some black individuals have a commercial relationship with nonblack domestic wholesalers. If there are no incentives for these wholesalers to give back to the community, they will not maintain such connections for the long term. I start to notice my outlook on China's economic development potential will not persuade colleagues to adopt an international strategy for micro-enterprises business opportunities. In particular, an approach creates an initiative for micro-enterprises to obtain direct access to the Chinese manufacturing sector. I remain hopeful sooner, rather than later; a local economic development office will decide to educate micro enterprises on how to manufacture or source products from China. And by such actions, I believe micro-enterprises will start to have an economic advantage over their present wholesalers because they will be able to attain fair and reasonable prices direct from Chinese factories. But then again, it's not easier undertaken to convince others to focus on an international business initiative to create an opportunity for black small business owners. I believe a chance to establish direct access to Chinese manufacturers for black individuals is a potential afterthought despite China's admission into the World Trading Organization. I am encouraged a business initiative can craft a competitive advantage to allow these business owners to have face-to-face contact with a Chinese manufacturer and product suppliers.

A competitive advantage because of some local municipalities, lack of international initiatives to overcome the business readiness barrier, prevent micro-enterprises from providing products and trade in services to benefit their community. The lack of readiness is unfortunate because I believe local economic development organization prefers to utilize tax dollars to support primary companies through retention and attraction of foreign and private investment. While on the other hand, they tend to pander support of micro-enterprises with programs promote various community development activities within their incorporated area of the city. In this case, primary companies receive foreign and private investment ought to solicit intermediate goods or services from micro-enterprises. In particular, if they produce a significant amount of imports from China with operations within China. And since most micro-enterprises are unaware intermediate goods or services are necessary for some primary business operation, they can import those products and provide an essential service to these primary businesses. I believe China's admission to the WTO in 2001 has an economic benefit for the black community with the proper support of micro-enterprises. The number of various products from children's toys to electronic devices imports from China will increase to meet consumer needs. With the admission of China into the WTO, micro-enterprises must be adept at advancing manufacture and market-ready products for global trade opportunities.

I have discussions with associates about how manufacture and market-ready products can support small size structures. Structures are ideal for small or micro-business development or entrepreneurial activities to include faith-based organizations and community development organizations. In like manner, I reckon some residential neighborhoods can have a large grocery store, pharmacy, restaurants, and other amenities to support their consumer needs. I listen to them about how like-minded black individuals have no economic relations with China, and key stakeholders will not play a significant role in formulating the sort of business relationship. Not to mention community development goals, objectives, and strategies create an economic development plan with a shared vision along with community ownership and buy-in. I start to realize some of these discussions focus on how to provide equitable job opportunities, better education curriculum, and not how to create economic equity with the greater China region for Black entrepreneurs.

Under these conditions, there is a need for me to elaborate on strategic economic equity partnerships between micro-enterprises and China. Because up to the present time, the local culture and politics, in particular, those with critical stakeholders who do not see the benefits as it relates to micro-enterprises. In the present analysis, I trust strategic stakeholders can align pivotal individuals to develop resources in the city to benefit micro-enterprises who desire to engage with China. The first thing to remember is likeminded micro-enterprises can collaborate with their Chinese counterparts to create potential business agreements. Agreements are built on the same mutual vision and not are one-sided due to the lack of cultural differences. By the same token in 2000-2001, I notice numerous business opportunities are suitable for micro-enterprises. I can appreciate when it comes to local community development plans, micro-enterprises need their manufacture and market-ready products ideas in the forefront to do direct business with China.

It's essential to realize as China continues to expand the manufacturing base and market-ready products, micro-enterprises will be in a position to reap those benefits. There should be subsidizing to permit micro-enterprises to receive the benefit of China manufacture and market-ready products for their customer base. I deem the allocation of grants will promote strategically position micro-enterprise growth to coincide with China manufacture and market-ready products for expansion is in local municipality best interest. Not only is it in the municipality's best interest, but I will also contend individuals with limited foreign business experience are in an awkward position to cease business agreements on an international scale. My discussions do yield any initiatives to realign support for micro-enterprises with the development of their overseas manufacturer and market-ready products for trade possibilities.

I begin to realize micro-enterprises with a desire to have a business relationship with China need adequate grants to educate them about the manufacturer and market-ready products for industry. I understand funds to train micro-enterprises about product information with which specific manufacturing agreements can be a lesser priority for local business officials. These micro-enterprises need sufficient foreign commercial service from their community development organization can increase their local competitive business opportunities. I notice when micro-enterprises want to set about a business in their local community, they realize their competitors have manufacture and brand products such as apparel, accessories, and consumer goods. Some will probe why they do not have access to these same products or how they can gain access to the manufacture like their competitors. To overcome the lack of access entrepreneurs will either drive to New York or Miami to purchase wholesale products from flea markets.

Some municipal development offices lack necessary groundwork to provide material for them to attend consumer electronics and appliances trade shows or visit foreign factories to acquire quality goods at fair and reasonable prices. They cannot source particular products such as medical equipment and medical care products to their black consumers. Micro-enterprises do not receive the type of technical assistance to meet their business goals. Within these situations, it is possible to transform segments of the classroom module so they can understand how to manufacture and source products from Chinese manufacturers and suppliers. I will maintain micro-enterprises can obtain practical skills to improve their supply chain network benefits from local tourism and hospitality industries. Some enterprises are capable of supporting new technologies; culture and education, or creative design consumers. I believe they must start trade-in service businesses and create sustainable jobs. By the same token, when micro-enterprises receive their equipment or supplies, they will expose them to the global economy. These innovative ideas require local development offices to adopt new classroom initiatives so micro-enterprises will be able to engage in the worldwide marketplace. They can change the narrative with expansion and exposure of manufacture, and market-ready products from techniques which will be necessary for them to compete within the local market. Couple the exposure to ocean freight, customs clearance, and local transportation; they can commence to develop their supply chain management team. Not only can micro-enterprises develop such a team, but they can also have a storefront to promote quality products to everyday consumers.

I conceive three classroom modules to instruct micro enterprises on how to develop manufacture and market-ready products for techniques with Chinese private industries. The first module creates strategies on how to identify business opportunities for micro-enterprises. The next will offer economic incentives to encourage collaboration among micro-enterprises and Chinese private manufacture and market-ready products for industries. And the final module focuses on cultural awareness, patience with the negotiation team, and the development of personal relationships. I consider classroom modules to encourage micro-enterprises to contact Chinese private businesses to support their business development for specific products and services suitable for the local community. Such support is whereby necessary because these businesses operate in economic development locations design to promote the tourism and hospitality industries. It is essential to have micro-enterprises in these locations to lessen their challenges when they attempt to provide competitive manufacture and source products to consumers. I think the local economic development office must support micro-enterprises with target growth initiatives, public funds, and federal capital investment. I will agree manufacture and market-ready products trade agreements between micro-enterprises and Chinese private industries benefits local communities. Only through the implementation of these three-classroom modules can an economic development concept, and other factors be utilized to energize micro-enterprises business opportunities.

Other factors benefit the black community through these modules, workforce development, and Chinese private industry connections are essential for sustainable black micro-enterprises. In the first place, these types of relationships require black micro-enterprises to take action now and think beyond local distributors for manufacture and source products. Not to mention activities utilize engagement with the Chinese private industry to improve its supply chain decision-making process in the long term. And through these decision-making processes, quality service builds strong strategic partnerships in the new economy. Here are a few suggestions for black micro-enterprises to communicate strategic business development with China. For the most part, build strong relationships, don't wait to the last minute, plan, improve inventory, get logistics right, plan for other options, and evaluate manufacturer and market-ready products for levels.

Perhaps one of the most thoughtful outcomes of these suggestions is they assist micro-enterprises to stay adaptable and be able to navigate the ever-changing landscape of global business. Insomuch micro-enterprises must adapt together so they can place themselves in a prime position to benefit from the globalization process. Some tend to build businesses, which need access to all sorts of advanced critical components to remain relevant. I believe here lies the problem with direct access to crucial elements. Micro-enterprises need to do what others haven't done nor had the interest to do. They have to identify a need, they have to find a niche, and they have to make it uniquely their own. It's an outcome for some may not be popular, but one speaks to the passivity lingers over the challenge of micro-enterprises allows them to thrive in the global economy.

Despite linger passivity, I recognize the potential problems of manufacturing and market-ready product troubles because micro-enterprises need to do what others haven't done within their business community. Most can provide pictures without a written description of their end product concept to illustrate what they want to create for the market. I suppose the problem with images is they rarely can identify which region can provide appropriate manufacture and product suppliers. In China, the different percentage of industries concentrate in any particular province ranges from thirty-three percent in the electronics industry from Guangdong to twenty percent in textiles from Jiangsu and thirty-two percent in the petrochemical industry from Shandong province. With such a diverse sector, especially in China, I tend to speculate on how to create a broader manufacturer distribution network for black businesses and to promote Black America's economic community abroad. The system of suitable leather and feather products manufacturers can benefit some Black American SMEs' economic growth. I realize China is immense and the manufacture of different types of products. Such products like a metal product come from Zhejiang, Guangdong, Jiangsu, Shandong, Hebei, Henan provinces is quite spread out. Given their lack of experience on how to develop their product specifications and requirements, micro-enterprise owners become passive about their market-ready product. While at the same time, they may not have mentors or practical resources in their local community to guide them in the right direction. Quite often, when some make an inquiry to the local business officials about how to manufacture and source products from China, they are often led to another agency to serve larger employers. Thereupon these small business owners receive inadequate resources, which inhibit their ability to compete as suppliers for target industries in such areas as healthcare services, business and information services, and light manufactures. To say nothing, does not put some small business owners' minds at ease because the perception is they lack awareness. It merely puts, in the long run, they must obtain familiarity on how to develop a supply chain network, which allows them to do what others haven't done. They cannot only rely on pictures are visual concepts of an end product. They will strive to create their product specifications and requirements and will not be insufficient because others have done it. In the final analysis, the sort of action is a potential manufacture and market-ready products problem for any micro-enterprise.

Due to the lack of direct access to foreign trade resources, some black entrepreneurs market-ready products undergo regular disadvantages. Aside from the potential problem, some achieve greatness even years after growth in the import and export industry. The development can be substantial differences between business partners, business opportunities, quality service, a small business coach, and practical skills to contribute to their business growth. As a consequence, supply chain management marks a new area for product development trade practices often used to explain or the need thereof with China. Yet it does not focus on how some black entrepreneurs need those same opportunities of international trade and mobility as it relates to the greater China region. In light of such requirements is black America has a constant legacy to encounter unrecognizable trade barriers within the United States. I believe without direct access to foreign manufacture and market-ready products; these entrepreneurs will remain at an economic disadvantage.

Not to mention how some formal classroom modules blunder because they attempt to bridge the knowledge gap with courses cover essential management, marketing, accounting and finance, and sales. Meanwhile, they offer no components on trade prospects and standards design to encourage economic growth projects for residents in the black community. Some black individuals may enjoy freedom as consumers and business owners. But unnecessary economic, cultural, judicial, and social issues target their community to distract them from the global marketplace. And since the possible purpose of disturbance is to inundate such difficulties into the black community so entrepreneurs cannot maintain profitable business models. Efficient classroom modules need to illustrate how to identify and then circumvent these challenges so economic growth can be access through the global economy. Maybe then others will take notice of new segments to utilize black intelligence to enhance global trade skills. In case, because of the improved insight into the worldwide marketplace, black businesspersons will invest in the process if the trend is big enough, they can capitalize on it. The method may be valid and despite all of the newfound awareness. I recognize some distractions' primary function is to restrict the "free flow of global business ideas," to prevent others from overcoming constraints.

5

Benefit From Constraints

I have to overcome constraints for specific import and export of wholesale and retail merchandise into the black community. The realization is I have to focus on particular merchandise with particular selection criteria, to understand which potential trade opportunity is more suitable for local merchants. I start to recognize the additional expertise can be pass onto other individuals and local stakeholders. I inform homegrown backers to offer the service to local merchants about which everyday use items they ought to sell to increase their competitive edge. In the same fashion, because of the resource, additional efforts to galvanize micro-enterprise growth will be an appropriate outcome. Community patrons with collaborative resources can be instrumental when they assist micro-enterprises to bypass specific national wholesalers, and retailers and create direct import of everyday use merchandise. The course of action negates the likelihood once disclose their competitors won't seek retaliation in the form of price reduction as a means to keep repetitive customers. They can conceal a slight profit lost with a lower price promotion to cause a decline in demand for black entrepreneurs goods because of a perception their merchandise is not competitive. But as black consumers demand their product increases despite lower prices, the requirement for import knowledge inside the black community must also increase. Another critical point is the demand for goods and services will not diminish, and the black American youth will increase their knowledge about the global economy. Given these points, I sought to discover new worldwide economic beneficial techniques to help advance the Black community's overall standard of living.

In a similar manner style, a supply chain management module for Black small and medium sized enterprises (SMEs) to manufacture and product source can enhance their business. The sort of proficiency will permit them to gain direct access to raw material and supplies are necessary for manufacturer purposes. I consider these to be an essential business element, and black buy movements and media channels will help spread the word. Profit margins will be higher since the supply chain management system allows SMEs to build and encourage other black retailer and wholesaler networks. And let's not forget Black-owned warehouses and tuckers will be necessary for a greater need to deliver merchandise to brick-and-mortar stores. I believe coupled global exposure and supply chain networks within SMEs, and particular entities will become more self-sufficient in the future. In the same fashion to do successful business with China, entrepreneurs need to identify a product or service benefits both parties. While at the same time, make sure their concept does not compete with the Chinese domestic market. And local counterfeiters must have no interest to duplicate or copy because it's not suitable for the Chinese domestic market. Despite these issues, there are not enough trade offices in China focus on Black American small business owners, and entrepreneurs attempt to engage in business opportunities. Even though some commercial services concentration is toward more giant corporations, they are not necessarily identical to smaller business entities' exposure to global trade prospects. The conversation needs to be in a context where SMEs can have mutually beneficial business opportunities even when there are commerce discussions about China trade negotiations.

The prominent black voices do not advocate for sustainable growth equity opportunities to amplify cooperatives with the greater China region. The amplification can explain the importance of Black America small business owners and entrepreneurs to interconnect with diverse foreign counterparts on global business issues. Besides the proper development of an advocacy group, their viewpoints can represent an additional form of cooperative efforts with China experts, media coverage, and on relevant discussion panels. The resurgence can cause black individuals to engage more with China and redevelop cooperation among other nations and people. Such individuals like Paul Robeson, W.E.B Du Bois, Vicki Garvin, Robert F. Williams, and Elaine Brown and Huey Newton cultivate Black America's connections as early as the 1930s as real friends to the people of China. As I go about to understand, these individuals moments to recognize China as a friend and reclaim their early admiration of Black America. To be sure, with renewal respect, I embark on lessening those common areas for Black entrepreneurs in their attempts to make trade agreements with their Chinese counterparts. Then again, the domestic market has become a consumption-driven economy from the time when China's demand for imports increases while exports decreases. These prominent voices must ignore excessive rhetoric about unfair trade practices and continue to persuade Black entrepreneurs to conduct direct business engagement with China. Not to mention, others will prepare themselves to benefit when the demand trend for export falls, prices of exportable goods inside China will also decline. Thereby Black entrepreneurs need to positionthemselves to reap profits when export prices are lower because direct access has two effects on rates: one tends to raise them; the other tends to lower them.

Some Black American SMEs struggle to minimize their risk when they attempt to manufacture and source products from foreign suppliers. For the most part, these owners want exposure to specific resources with as little complications as possible. It can be as simple as an affordable seminar describes how to prepare product specifications and requirements for their end products. If unavailable, then the black business community will require their local economic development office to include the conference in their budget. Within the particular monetary context, business growth and development will bring about deeper entrepreneur awareness into the manufacturer and product source process. I think a market-ready merchandise design concept includes information about Pantone color arrangement, raw material composite, logo design, and product function, and package layout. Not only the knowledge but also pinpoint which purpose of their product use lacks difficulty and ensures their customers have the best experience.

I hope some business owners will establish a supply chain system to support workforce development for their projects. The management system can transition from an immediate, too long-term business growth strategy for specific trade opportunities with other counterparts. One such particular intermediate area can be to identify and minimize delivery delays for specific functional components necessary to provide a quality product. It is to say; confident black entrepreneurs will use due diligence to maintain large and complex supply chain management skills when needed. I believe the required business skills will lead to a labor-intensive workforce to compliments global trade, particularly for black individuals, who won't feel left out in the cold. Of course, the skill set alone won't drive a substantial black workforce to the global supply chain system unless black businesses participate in the worldwide marketplace. In essence, they can start to change the narrative about black employment through proper extensive connections focus on the supply chain system.

One change area is unfamiliar trade barriers are an occurrence for small black business owners and entrepreneurs when they attempt to engage in the global economy. I suppose others tend to ignore how some entrepreneurs encounter trade difficulties in such areas as payment methods, quality insurance, logistical support, design concepts, custom clearance, and language barriers. Black American SMEs are inclined to acknowledge the formation of successful end products partnership with foreign manufacture and product source representatives. Such development with these individuals who identify themselves as international colleagues will not get notable recognition within the black community. As such, for all intent purposes, the norm is to provide distractive media content and not international trade opportunities to black entrepreneurs. And in return, the belief is to have enough industry resources to access the global economy. When in fact, I am mindful of five subsequent suggestions to better position Black SMEs

1.   Always research manufacture and supplier location for your merchandise
2.   Base your decision on as many facts as possible about which manufacture and supplier can deliver your end creation

3. Surround yourself with similar-minded individuals who have foreign manufacture and supplier insights
4. Visit and observe the manufacture and supplier environment yourself
5. Maintain awareness about which manufacture and supplier are doing well and those not performing so well

Even though the above suggestions may not be appropriate for some entrepreneurs, they illustrate my experiences for others to utilize with their trade platforms to source market-ready products. Some trade platforms can be less complicated for those with extensive knowledge of how to input their product descriptions and requirements. While for others, it can be more problematic because they are less familiar with these platforms, and they submit vague depiction via their search requirements. In either situation, merchandise explanation and needs might include other areas such as material composition, color scheme, and internal/external components for adequate manufacture and source products. Not only do I have to handle promotion, customer service, and other internal departments, I also need direct access to foreign manufacturers or suppliers. And if not, I need to decide if it's practical to outsource the function to meet my customer demands. I will have to validate these manufacturers and suppliers comply with international trade guidelines and policies. Even so, most black small business owners lack such expertise on how to utilize Chinese B2B trade platforms to transmit suitable methods of communication with their foreign counterparts on a periodical basis. Their interaction, for the most part, manifests on purchases of market-ready products already meet import and export establish product and service standards. SMEs must have the necessary competence, so when the time comes for their particular product to meet such global standards, they'll be ready.

In terms of short and long term development, some entrepreneurs hold onto the notion of any attempt to present their idea to the global marketplace can result in inconsistent products and inadequate service from their efforts. So as a defense mechanism, they tend to latch onto the sense it's more beneficial to utilize individual resources and invest in well-known customer brand items for resale to their clients. Not the mention, some of these items tend to provide them with the self-assurance they will increase their return on investment (ROI), and they won't be overwhelmed with debt. In such situations, some entrepreneurs might believe they will make less profit if they were to manufacture their products. Of course, this exists when particular SME owners have no exposure to global original equipment manufacturer (OEM), original brand manufacture (OBD) and original design manufacturer (ODM) in their business growth plan. I imagine each foreign trade office needs to intertwine skills among economic development planners, procurement officers, warehouse operators, customs broker, and truck driver will help bring supply chain efficiency to SME owners.

I believe black entrepreneurs will be able to provide quality products and services are necessary to gain confidence with direct access to the global marketplace. Although it may not be proven, they must overcome numerous distractions and demonstrate how to facilitate new global trade agreements. Not only will such trade agreements have a significant growth impact on their bottom line, but they can also become importers into the largest country of consumption. Within the next forthcoming years, the number of goods and services from imports these SMEs can commence to standardize a new global trade agreement. In 1978, when China adopts its reform and opening-up policy, the black American business community did not propose direct engagement tactics for substantial growth opportunities with China. In the short-term, numerous trade barriers are removable, contribute to the lack of engagement for black entrepreneurs with China. As such, it is foreseeable to establish a black American trade organization for the long-term focus on areas of trade such as investment and tourism and trade in goods and services in China.

Without both of these necessary actions, the black community will continue to rely on "buy black" campaigns and mount mass campaigns to force concessions from government and white-controlled corporations. As a consequence, I believe five reasons can explain the low numbers of Black entrepreneurs engage in the global marketplace. The first is young Blacks have less exposure to entrepreneurial role models in the global economy. Next is some Black entrepreneur has fewer informal and formal global networks to secure critical resources and information. The third is less direct access to foreign manufacturers and suppliers. The fourth reason is classroom modules do not provide "practical experience" and global business exposure. The final is too many local economic development offices tend not to have the proper resources to develop their international business programs.

As a consequence, there will be an initiative to develop resources to interlink these reasons into a Black American SME empowerment model. A model focuses on mobilizing social, financial, and institutional stakeholders to assist in the growth of SMEs' business opportunities in two ways. The first is to offer modules on how to access global business opportunities, and the second is to provide economic incentives to encourage collaboration with their foreign counterparts. I think it's necessary to merge external factors between public-private investment (PPI), local SMEs, and product and service industries. First of all, regional business development initiatives between PPI and SME can change towards more straightforward products and services based commercial relationships.

For one thing, PPI and SMEs can improve better fiscal oversight based on their community's competitive advantages in the marketplace regardless of location. I think the monitoring will change the generalization of economic equity has significant implications for local SMEs and outside competitors. In this case, the financial investment will allow absolute autonomy of decision-making for products and services based commercial relationships. The relationship between public funds and SME will change because economic equity will promote business subsidies, and the private sector will be responsible for business development out of their budget. The Black American SME is an essential commercial entity because it will introduce their products and services to target inner-city neighborhoods. The business development products and trade in functions will operate through a fair distribution of financial responsibility between local government, private-owned units, and small and medium sized enterprises. The equitable distribution of equity is necessary to promote the commercialization of global business development for those SMEs who do not have direct access to international institutions.

Most community development office does not utilize existing laws and regulation for SMEs to engage with the global marketplace; they instead patronize them for their local products and services. I believe the solution is to ensure municipalities embrace relation generates sufficient revenue to fund business development projects. The prerequisite is necessary because I think many local community development offices exert pointless controls over Black American SMEs' business development process to preclude their growth within their local areas. I believe in establishing a balanced and healthy business market, any business projects get support from the local municipality, and private investment is necessary to include local small and medium enterprises. The exclusionary practice is not essential because one of the main objectives for Black American SME is to covert its marketable products and trade in services to domestic and worldwide buy-ins development projects. The benefit of economic equity is base on community development projects existence where products and services consideration will be more prominent. Which offers a better alternative than black neighborhoods become a casualty without the presence of Black Small and medium sized enterprises.

6

Other Than Through

I sense Black America needs specific foreign trade advocates for business prospects other than through American movies, the Internet, and American television media outlets. I n particular, with access to China's private industries, how to accomplish it, there tends to be a scarcity of information. I am not sure if others contemplate; instead, a noble cause is necessary to pursue business with China. As such, I fandom some may rely on Black American movies, the Internet, and American television media outlets to offer opinions before they can formulate their own about China. I feel if there is not an opportunity for black media to express such an idea, then there will be one. Some media outlets influence me, as an adolescent, to imitate Bruce Lee Kung Fu movements. I acknowledge my decent version of those physical gestures were, in some way, an expression of acceptance about Chinese culture. Between 2000-2001, as a guest to Mainland China, I became aroused by another cross-cultural situation has a profound impact on inspirational possibilities. The possibility a significant black student population will participate in study abroad programs in China. Within my circle of family and friends, there is an unimaginable perception a considerable amount of individuals will not partake in the program. Whereas, I believe we need individuals who recognize how the black community can benefit when HBCU students participate in such endeavors. I did not know the venture gives me first-hand exposure to an overseas global economic development initiative with Chinese characteristics. The possibility to identify where international trade resources are will be of benefit to the black community other than through fickle media outlets.

Exposure to Mainland China has some similarities to my study interest in the role of migrant workers in the economic development of China. I prefer the research interest because of it resemblances the movement of Black Americans in the U.S. between 1916 and 1970, known as The Great Migration. I believe the migration of about six million Negroes from the rural south to the urban northeast, mid-west, and western part of the United States. Similar in 1978, China's Open Door Policy inspires migrant workers from the countryside to urban areas to reveal a recognizable movement pattern. Within the movement, I obtain a chance to acquire first-hand knowledge about the country encourages me to seek out a standard beneficial connection between Black America and China. The first-hand recognition without limitation only involves Bruce Lee movies or a local Chinese eatery. The lack of a typical relationship is not because our business institutions did not specify additional information about China much less about the Chinese private industry. I believe there is a likelihood black business owners, chamber organizations, and black students are susceptible to accept mainstream media destructive commerce notions about China. From a hands-on perspective, the unfamiliar with China's business system can give credence for the mindset since black entrepreneur needs assistance from an establishes foreign trade office. I wonder if their dilemma will become apparent since there are endless possibilities to expand with opportunities in China. For black entrepreneurs, it's conceivable to partner with the Chinese private industry despite deceptive imagines from

American movies, the Internet, and American television media outlets.

I believe deceptive media tactics are attempts to fuel suspicion and cultural stereotypes continue to separate China and Black America to seek business collaboration. The absence of interpersonal contact between Mainland China and Black America is pervasive under the current situation. As such, I notice research about stereotypes of Black Americans and media use among Chinese high school students. As social learning predicts, we can expect respondents' stereotypes of Americans in general and Black Americans, in particular, to be influenced by movies, television, and the print media via processes of vicarious learning. Media portrayals of Black Americans determine the direction of influence. American media harms stereotypes because, as previous research has shown, Black Americans have a negative representation in American media.

On the other hand, the Chinese media do not portray Black Americans negatively. When Black Americans are featured, they are usually shown as victims of poverty or protesting for civil rights. Chinese audiences will form positive perceptions about Black Americans when they see a Chinese person they identify with positive interaction and cooperation with Black Americans to pursue a common goal. The expected use of Chinese media can predict the positive stereotypes of Black Americans.

It's possible when I connect with Chinese private industries to develop business opportunities; my economic strength will grow. I can go about securing global business agreements to enhance commercial solutions for the betterment of the black community. In China, some collaborative opportunities are oblivious to black business owners because they lack exposure to the local marketplace. I'm optimistic more Black American entrepreneurs want to explore their business model with Chinese private industries. A collaborative partnership group business activities focus on producers and suppliers and create jobs. Through the formation of positive media perceptions in China, black inventors of products and service providers can contribute to the world community. A community of inventors includes products like consumer electronics and appliances, apparel, accessories and consumer goods, and the the automobile high-end intelligent equipment. Also, food and agricultural products, medical equipment and medical care products, and trade in services are suitable for global consumption. I once sought to build upon China's media perception and start to become more proactive with global business collaborative enterprises. I consider the creation of sustainable media organizations in China to focus on such business awareness is a great project. A media insight promotes how the black community will no longer domesticate itself into inequality, but tames itself into the global economy. As such, I start to support a local media initiative for black business growth opportunities as the sole channel for products or services within the greater China region.

An initiative I believe promotes awareness about black entrepreneurs need to use and leverage their dominant knowledge power with Chinese private entities. Leverage through mutual partnerships demonstrates support and commitment to the betterment of their business community. These partnerships can embrace trade events with media outlets value them as knowledge-based producers. This isalled reciprocity. I'm mindful China creates an unprecedented collection of global trade events for participants to examine trade-related information with more businesses from different countries and territories. In these trade events, an individual can gain a better perspective on the latest supply and demand trends for internationally traded products and services. I seldom encounter black media platforms with a specific focus to promote Black America's trade representative business identity and interest in China. I contemplate what sort of media distraction is so prevalent Black American business organizations will be oblivious to trade developments in China. Maybe their lack of interest is due to insufficient trade information as to what business prospect occurs in China. I feel there ought to be media organizers in the greater China region-specific to inform Black America trade delegation about trade events. These media organizations' effectiveness will depend on the ability to receive suitable material in sufficient time.

It's my experience related trade show events through local organizations do not reach black business stakeholders allow appropriate time to form a global trade team. If it did, I believe a Black America trade team consists of businesswomen, businessmen, and startups will have collective projects to access the greater China region. Thereby they can generate prospects to develop and then implement international trade agreements for the black American community. I know it's favorable when overseas trade groups from such countries like Ghana, Nepal, Togo, Tonga, Belarus, Uganda, Pakistan, Myanmar, Kenya, Panama, and Uzbekistan participate in import and export trade events to understand Chinese consumers. In particular, for me to acknowledge the growth in trade show participants is no coincidence due to the sizable amount of foreign and domestic trade offices throughout China. I recognize the challenge for some business owners are which trade shows to attend when there are no specific media organizations in China represent their interest. It's a common challenge for these business owners because if they want to do business in China, they must have some media presence in China. I consider once black media entrepreneurs are diligent in establishing a presence in China, the execution of sustainable agreements will give them a foothold with a Chinese manufacturer and product trade show providers. But, it's unfortunate; stateside black entrepreneurs continue to receive American media perspectives; there are no business incentives to engage in China.

Advance notification about specific trade shows is a vital media tool for black business owners to introduce their innovative products or services in China. They need to understand Chinese consumers so they can get down to create innovative products and services to appeal to them. Which individual does not mean Chinese consumers will only accept domestic products. It means they need to offer a product or service benefits both parties; they do not compete with local companies and are not easy to duplicate. Black American entrepreneurs do not get enough inside media coverage to understand what it means China's economy is more open, which is a positive message for businesses everywhere. For those business owners who do not realize China is no longer the world's factory; instead, it's a fast-growth consumer market. In 2007, when I wander around several stylish and exclusive shops on significant streets and small lanes during my leisure time, I'm sensing the flavor of black culture. I have the perception Chinese youth tends to appreciate the hustle and flow personality of our culture. Some business is not only enrichment to their integrity, but also a black theme because it is a kind of subtle practices, a black culture lifestyle practice. Instead, through song, hipster fashion, sports icon, global influencers, and dance, it is the black experience theme to push some Chinese people to embrace Black Americans.

I sense China will become to be one of the countries with have the largest middle class on the globe. For me, three implications emerge from potential growth. First, it is vital to view Chinese youth as part of a global economic system. Give Black American child opportunities can link their commonalities with an upcoming Chinese youth population. I believe less attention will be given to their particular domestic location, especially if their sites are exclusive within America's low-moderate income neighborhoods. Their commonalities can forge strong links between Black America and Chinese youth into significant, more extensive global partnerships. Second, I am encouraged business partnerships among Black American SMEs and Chinese private industries are useful. On the practical side, black foreign trade offices and black overseas media outlets can explore how to promote collaboration between Black American SMEs and Chinese private industries in the below five areas.

1. Specific how trade groups will pursue supplier contracts.
2. Develop joint ventures and co-ventures agreements.
3. Create strategic alliances and subcontracts between Black American SMEs and Chinese private industries.

4. Establish information clearinghouses, roundtables, and business directories.
5. Develop virtual overseas incubation programs tied to Black American SMEs and Chinese private sectors.

Third, foreign entrepreneurs need to create unique and different products or somewhat change products to attract Chinese buyers. As such, Black American entrepreneurs must resist the temptation to confine their business development activities and programs exclusive to the United States. It is unfortunate some individuals or organizations naivety tends to impose trade barriers to prevent capable black business owners from benefiting from the international market. When practiced, it only reinforces their business isolation to residential areas and from the global economy.

My experience to assists these entrepreneurs lacks media focus on the removal of obstacles to their success, irrespective of their business geographic location and with an orientation toward direct access to a Chinese manufacturer and private industries. I imagine direct access to Chinese private sectors is the greatest need for Black American SME who wants to redevelop low-moderate neighborhoods. They have a vital role in how to create jobs and nurture human capital for the black community. After the Open Door Policy, it makes little sense to limit Black American SME activities and business partnerships to the confinement of the United States. A broader economic scope requires the collaboration of Black American SMEs with Chinese private media industries to promote trade events through Black America's financial wealth. A partnership plan not only solidifies economic growth potential; but also quantifies products and services appeal to local consumers, distribution partners, and e-commerce platforms for success.

I wonder if Black America recognizes media distractions target China's competitive edge in specific manufacturer industries but overshadows its competitive advantage in particular service industries. For me, China provides new channels to strengthen business cooperation and promote the shared prosperity of the world economy and trade. And since I have been in Shanghai for quite some time, it has become one mega business center for the worldwide economy. Particular in industries where Black Americans can obtain business prospects with other countries, regions, and international organizations. A business community will attend trade events in China with local media coverage to promote their business acumen. I believe Black America is more competitive when engaging in partnerships with the greater China region. We need to participate in trade in service opportunities in such areas as new energy vehicles, artificial intelligence, and the Internet industries to formulate trade agreements. In 2018, I noticed Black American commerce organizations, after forty years since Open Door Policy, do not have a present foothold in China. For substantial economic growth with the black community, these business organizations need to have direct engagement channels with Chinese private industries. I believe they can remove numerous hidden barriers if their members sought to enter China in such areas as trade, investment, tourism, and trade in services. I imagine there ought to be some sort of foreign trade advocacy with enormous business opportunities to support their accumulation into China.

7

Generate Trade Agreements

In light of various import and export projects, I sense the manufacture and product source aspect of these endeavors can generate more business collaboration in China. Notwithstanding, local strategies which promote inward growth for low-moderate neighborhood residences, it's outside competitors' who tend to benefit from development opportunities. Black American small business owners from these communities can have a competitive advantage through the generation of trade agreements with Chinese private industries. I believe some municipalities rely on state organizations to make commerce inroads which benefit large companies but minimize potential business connections between SMEs and Chinese private sectors. I recognize these agencies lack the tendency to inform localities that overseas manufacturers and suppliers can be a source to improve economic conditions for low-moderate income neighborhoods. It will be a more viable option for municipalities to implement foreign manufacture and product source modules for SMEs in these neighborhoods. I foresee manufacture and product source industries will have a profound strategic change for these community residences. A strategic shift of a municipal economic development function can focus on practical projects for SMEs to generate trade agreements with overseas partners. With the change, in turn, it will identify which Chinese private industries and Black American SME can negotiate on mutual beneficial projects. I sense the involvement of Chinese private sectors is essential to expand together and develop a shared interest in practical projects with small and medium sized enterprises. The need for expansion can go beyond the consumers' concept and become a model to push their businesses into the global economy.

Before 2005, I did not know how to do business in and with Chinese private industries. I deem through various cooperative partnerships; I acquire insight on why international agreements between Black American SMEs and the greater China region can advance within a three-phase process. The first phase is where SME can participate in collective outreach modules with specific Chinese private industries. It includes the acquisition of recollected insights with their local colleagues through foreign counterparts for beneficial agreements. They will utilize practical assignments to understand multifaceted manufacturing and product source projects. Throughout the period, I share incremental achievements in the Chinese production and service industries with colleagues. The awakening phase includes educational and alternative forms of business development initiatives. These initiatives involve model trade agreements with Chinese private sectors in areas of trade in services, cultural products, and environmental issues. These models include the ability to source and reproduce goods increase the opportunity for economic growth. The final phase is the holistic phase involves trust, respect, and cooperation to share the benefits and challenges insight of international commercial partnerships. I realize the phrase will be problematic because it requires municipalities to implement a manufacturing and product source strategy—a strategy to create collaborative projects to benefit inner-city neighborhood entrepreneurs to expand through China's private industries.

There is little evidence a Black America foreign trade office development strategy exists in the greater China region. I did not grasp the importance of the specific absence resource until after an invitation to engage in foreign trade prospects came from a Chinese colleague. I had no practical experience or guidelines on how to source, manufacture, and import and export products from China. The existence of a foreigner entrepreneur community with various outreach programs to improve foreign trade skills is null and void in Shanghai. In 2005, to seek out any international organization to focus exclusively on Black America's economic growth with China is nonexistent. Even for any stateside black chamber organizations, their presence does not exist in Mainland China. For me to witness these probable outcomes cause a great deal of frustration because I did not want to squander the possibility to understand foreign trade while in China. I feel such resources will assist others in acquiring those necessary materials and supplies for business growth. To my astonishment, I receive an offer to bring awareness about such resources in China to these individuals.

A partnership offer came to me about four years after China's entry, the World Trade Organization (WTO) for international trade and commerce. Even though I lack direct access to foreign investment entities in China, I receive a proposal from a Wenzhou counterpart to establish a Mainland China import and export company. The company will fill a void where large organizations lack common interest to support stateside small and medium sized enterprises. Standard benefits are supportive of foreign firms in various investment activities such as automotive, agriculture, textile, and distribution/retail markets. I figure within the organization; I can enlighten Black American SMEs on how to benefit from China trade and commerce industry through import and export opportunities. I understand for individuals who want a business relationship with China; it's paramount they have a pathway to support their interest. I ponder how to present a beginner's approach will bring foreign trade agreements to these particular entrepreneurs. The types of trade projects will provide them practical experience on how to source, manufacture, and import and export worldwide products.

Through my position, I ensure the import and export company implement an outreach program for these black entrepreneurs. I understand Black America business community must explore different ways to develop and expand economic ties with China. I am cautious within the process large foreign and domestic organizations will not educate Black American SMEs on the economic benefits of trade with China. As such, I recognize stateside Black American SMEs without a physical presence or trade advocate in China can receive insufficient business opportunities. Not to mention, what happens in the import and export industry can expand business opportunities between Black American SMEs and Chinese private sectors. I became aware of the manufactured product for textile items centers on the design concept, material selection, and packaging methods in areas of production, service, and cost and duty taxes. Some project requires me to coordinate import and export schedules for SMEs from Chinese factory door to port of departure to port of entry. The strategy I sometimes encounter is clients and manufacturer has delivery expectation based on their own business experiences. While at the same time, they were well informed about our business experience and not to discredit each other's lack of knowledge about the other's business experiences. To lessen trade issues between Black American SME,

Chinese manufacturers, and the import and export company, I learn how to utilize China's business resources. I attain a set of skills to complete the task through supply chain networks made deliverables successful under international trade practices. The skillset includes visits to factories and suppliers throughout China with colleagues to specify project expectations for the import and export company. To visit factories are necessary to eradicate underline problems occurrence with quantity amount, material specification, shipping marks, and packaging method.

I do more to assist Black entrepreneurs in generating international and domestic trade agreements. Through my numerous visits, I observe there's a shortage of informed people who can advocate for Black American SMEs to create trade agreements with Chinese private businesses. I'm concerned the deficit appears to have two unknown factors in nurturing sustainable support for SMEs to develop international commercial contracts. I believe Black America needs to understand why there's an advantage to generate trade with the Chinese private industry. China's private sector needs to know how to create a business with Black America. I figure a new collaborative organization can connect the how and why difference to generate trade agreements. I imagine a holistic approach to Black business development with Chinese private industries can involve a two-way ideology of shared interest and mutual benefits for economic growth. These shared beliefs can focus on strategic agreements with everyday used items, and science and technology projects to benefit Black American SMEs and the Chinese private industry. I believe these strategic agreements will be pathways for overseas commercial collectives to support black businesses. At most, they can minimize trade barriers hinder stateside black collectives' ability to become profitable entities. I imagine with these changes; the local black business group will concentrate on creation, expansion, and retention of specific commercial activities for their neighborhood. Besides, business groups' focus on particular industries can pool financial, commercial, and educational resources with Chinese private sectors. From my experience, I recognize there are possible restraints applicable to some black organizations within a specific county or local municipality. These limitations may be ingrain in civil procedures to favor others' interests rather than support commercial expansions to marginalize populations. A holistic approach for black business realignment with Chinese private industries can achieve possible growth patterns. In particular, when import and export orders reveal, Black American SME products and services can generate foreign and domestic trade agreements.

I suppose one possibility is to assist SME from the low-to-moderate community with a population of sixty percent black, twenty-seven percent white, and thirteen percent Hispanic with business growth. If the possibility does not favor the populace group, then educate SME on how to manufacture and source products. The purpose is to inform them so they can position themselves to create commerce contracts in case there are opportunities to become material and supply contractors. I think these localities can promote SME as their chosen local material and supply contractors. The probable business expansion within low-moderate neighborhoods can be vital in the redevelopment of these communities. Once SME is inclusive of local improvement ventures, they can become primary stakeholders to expand regional growth.

On the other hand, SMEs, if they choose, can limit outside competitors to come in and create industries theoretical in their neighborhoods. I feel a measurable process to execute the common-sense approach will determine if it favors particular communities. The potential issue with the situation depends on rather or not Black American SMEs have the support of local stakeholders. For example, municipalities want to provide small business owners with innovative educational modules to create and sustain their businesses in a competitive market. They set about to take inventory on which companies can serve both public and private industries in their local community. I expect the process will reveal a different gap in product and trade-in service functions commercial engagement from low-moderate entrepreneurs. Even with awards of earmark funds through governmental policies and among other private agreements complement their local business community. The question then becomes how municipalities can support these potential entrepreneurs when they want to engage themselves in their local market. I feel the underline approach is how to assist entrepreneurs in accessing foreign manufacturers, and product providers are more suitable for growth in their niche business. An available module through practical projects for young black American entrepreneurs from these neighborhoods to involve themselves in various industries to help benefit their communities.

The practical project is an eye-opener for black entrepreneurs to position themselves to reap the benefits for the black community. It is not an educational module to just benefit a few and where the majority of black individuals are workers. I explore practical projects where tangible results for small Black business engagement compliment their overseas counterparts. I am not sure on a domestic level; specific programs exist to support them to manufacture and source products. To combat the issue, they can look at those end items' point of departure to ascertain their country of origin. The procedure allows them to learn how to identify distributors and foreign suppliers of import items into their area. Small and medium sized enterprises will learn how to deal with the import and export market so they will grow their business. It makes no sense to suggest the only way for Black American SMEs to grow their business is to focus on their domestic market. I set in motion to look at inner-city neighborhood corridors; I think how a low-moderate income person can develop a business on those strips. I know, for some, it is the right thing to do as a process to secure their economic future. Other entrepreneurs have another procedure. I think they must unlearn and relearn how to establish direct business relationships with overseas manufacturers and product suppliers. I know it's essential for them to understand how to generate foreign trade agreements to be competitive in their local market. In the same fashion, they need to know which foreign counterpart will provide long-term benefits for their business development.

I sense SMEs receive adequate guidance from municipalities about domestic resources to develop their local trade. But they receive improper access from them to build their overseas collaborations. A collaborative approach requires a thorough evaluation to access those resources, which can offer the most benefits. When I communicate with clients, and they tell me I have a lot of business experiences with Chinese private industries. I say, "We can obtain practical experience with China regardless of our educational and professional background in one way or another." China is the second leading economy, and it only makes sense to understand the country if we want to know how to manufacture and source products from the Chinese private industries to better our economic condition in America." I do understand SMEs want to know how to get merchandise from China based on my experience. I desire to give back as much awareness as I can and share with others how a "Leap of Faith" allows me to receive the knowledge. I believe it's a necessity to give back so others can reap the benefits of my China experiences, and then they can pass it on. They can understand how hands-on knowledge will inspire others. When I evaluate manufacture and product providers who can help small black-owned businesses grow and expand in the worldwide market. I have to admit it's a challenge to make sure these entrepreneurs are in a position to generate trade agreements. Black entrepreneurs need to access different resources in China and then apply them to help their business within America. These two elements, access and resource have to coexist; they are vital to the economic growth within the black community.

I recognize revitalization projects for product and trade-in service comes from derelict residential and commercial corridors surrounding black communities. These corridors have a higher percentage of vacant buildings and thousands of square feet of empty building space. They also include several buildings with collapsed roofs, which can lead to the perception of crime-ridden areas. With the ability to access overseas manufacturing and product suppliers for economic expansion projects, SMEs may start to implement symbolic endeavors as a means to revitalize these areas. I imagine Black entrepreneurs can create grassroots efforts such as paint crosswalks, striping bike lanes, and install planters and bike racks. I reckon Black American SMEs will benefit more from inner-city revitalization projects because they have direct access to specific line items. For most inner-city neighborhood small business owners, they need to implement a supply chain network for particular line items. With their accessibility to overseas manufacturers and product suppliers, these business owners can go about to transform their community into sustainable residential and commercial districts. They must acquire extensive practical experience like others so they can start to engage in neighborhood commercial corridor revitalization projects. Once Black American SMEs receive direct access to proper resources, then they will have enough confidence to make a considerable difference. I think about various trade events in China, even though some black individuals may not have direct access to them, they offer an alternative view about international trade. My concerns are how to make them aware of actual start times for these events. I mean, for black entrepreneurs — black expo organizers and participants—in the buy black mindset, but not ready to engage because of perceiving cultural predisposition with Chinese manufactures and product suppliers. I am aware of the presumptions Black America may face when attempts are to do business with Chinese private industries. These opinions are the same inherent notion a black-own or black-affiliate manufacture, and product source provider will have poor quality control, unskilled workers, inconsistent deliveries, and a host of other undesirable elements.

I am attentive to others harbor the notion of the possible neighborhood in which the business function, the clientele they serve, or their very race will be harmful and detrimental to potential business growth. Fortunately, I have experience in how to access resources with Chinese private industries to generate trade agreements. Even if one deal does not apply to one specific black community, it does not mean the overview agreement cannot apply to other black communities. I believe there is an exact and ominous faction to condition other people, races, and cultures to imagine the worst about black business owners and employees. Because no matter how many well-organized black-owned businesses exist, their firsthand ability will test once they go about to deliver various items to supplementary companies.

I believe Black entrepreneurs can retail and wholesale quality adult care products, everyday used items, household items, children's toys, non-electronic toys, and tools & hardware to inner-city communities. The biggest problem is they have not stimulated corporate retail and wholesale programs with a global manufacturer and product suppliers, in particular, Chinese private industries. While individuals from other cultures benefit from their unique clique of product and services, inner-city commercial corridors can become an ideal location for black business growth in the same way. Their storefronts can retail and wholesale artistic mural supplies to different places where pedestrians can stop and take selfless on an open space. I recognize black entrepreneurs will have others to question their abilities to boast a plethora of local black-owned businesses. They can provide holistic restaurants and stores are a bustle with outside patrons. There is a particular type of businesspeople will like to see on their block will make them spend more time there. The solution for Black

American SMEs is to access foreign manufacture and product providers to make it easier for their business expansion. I consider when Black entrepreneurs see more business opportunities per square feet of empty building space; they will know those areas can cultivate new residential or commercial space.

For some black businesses to renovate, they will require material and supplies from their overseas counterparts. Once in possession of such items, worthy things will happen. The difference involves more practical projects, which allows SMEs to gain access to a Chinese manufacturer and product suppliers to become more competitive as small business owners. Despite these differences between the domestic and overseas providers, Black American SMEs in inner-city neighborhoods converge in three clusters for the black community: (1 poor understanding of the manufacture and product source process, (2 ineffective strategy to engage with foreign manufacturers and suppliers, and (3 under performance in import and export operation and execution. The underline problem for Black American SME to participate in neighborhood revitalization programs is the absence of an overseas supply chain network. A sustainable linkage engages entrepreneurs to generate trade agreements with Chinese manufacturers and suppliers for the betterment of low-moderate income neighborhoods.

I believe community development programs target entrepreneurs in low-moderate income areas for community development is necessary. Still, I think they do not provide them common knowledge to develop their retail and wholesale supply chain. The lack of experience for the particular business function places these entrepreneurs in an awkward position. It allows outside competitors to be retail and wholesale those necessary commercial items into Black American SME communities. External competitors' retail and wholesale practice affects the economic base within black communities because they are keen to maintain their supply chain network. I foresee they can preserve a commercial advantage through silence since no black entrepreneur has challenged their competitive advantage. One possible way to test their silence is to target Black American SMEs to require economic development officials to provide accessible overseas retail and wholesale manufacturers and product suppliers. Once SMEs undertake their retail and wholesale operation by assessing Chinese private industries for reasonable merchandise, they can capitalize on their competitive advantages. Even though local economic development partners' actions dictate, it's better to do domestic business. Since most owners can conclude, they have favorable business development prospects with regional contractual agreements. The black entrepreneur business model for the inner city needs access to worldwide merchandise. I believe direct access to international suppliers will always challenge the status quo because outside competitors are shield from personal effects by it.

Potential entrepreneurs can attend conferences and trade events for good ideas can spark an immediate business interest. To develop a business, they need to diminish certain limitations for a retail and wholesale supply chain network. The problem they can encounter is not which occasions they can attend, but how to look beyond their present-day restriction for business prospects. I conceive retail and wholesale merchandise for a personal service industry like application software developer, medical service manager, construction laborer, registered nurse, medical technologist, and yoga instructors can launch into countless commerce prospects. The problem exists where potential Black American SMEs do not know how to provide these items inside their immediate areas. I suspect potential entrepreneurs who are employees in jobs such as dishwashers; childcare workers; cashiers; host and hostesses; amusement park attendants, farmworkers, and personal and home care aides have a responsibility to their employers. These entrepreneurs can have limited resources, limit foreign travel experience, and the sole obligation to cover their expenses. But given a chance to attend conferences and trade events within their immediate area can ignite a retail and wholesale business interest. I believe Chinese private industries present a unique linkage to support Black American SMEs as their official source for access to retail and wholesale merchandise.

There are business conferences and trade events in China to offer black entrepreneurs direct access to the Chinese market. These occasions provide inroads to practical merchandise allow small business owners and entrepreneurs to engage in import and export opportunities. Comparable projects with Chinese counterparts can introduce specific business groups' focus on the black business community. I consider attendance in business conferences and trade event a vital obligation on Mainland China to develop Black American trade organizations. I experience bilateral trade agreements through these occasions with diverse access to raw material, appropriate manufacture and supplier, freight forwarder, customs broker, and local transporter providers. Access to Mainland China resources is well within these essential areas to generate trade agreements. Some import and export organizations have roots in the local business culture but are not business liaison for the black community. I recognize black small business owners and entrepreneurs have limited resources to generate overseas trade agreements, which depends on strategic foreign partnerships. These strategic collaborations are necessary for the expansion of the Black American SME manufacturer and product supplier relationship in the greater China region.

8

Domestic Trade Organizations

I feel various Black American SMEs cannot specify significant business growth when access to the foreign manufacturer and product suppliers is not through domestic chamber organizations. Most Black America chamber organizations provide members with direct access to Black business leaders throughout the Black business community. They provide members with opportunities to hear guest speakers on a variety of significant subjects and participate in relevant ethnic, educational, and political events. Some have benefited include workshops and seminars design to assist Black American SMEs and entrepreneurs to bid on solicitations from stateside government and private corporations. I envision these chambers may not receive a substantial amount of overseas trade agreement prospects with foreign trade prospects. In particular, within the Greater China regional allows direct access to Chinese private industries can benefit their membership. I suppose it is not the fault of these Black Chamber organizations to lack direct access to foreign trade opportunities, as much it is the fault of those institutes with access but fails to share the knowledge. If the pattern persists, it gives consent to those institutions to continue in fashion. I feel it's an unfortunate situation when black entrepreneurs encounter resistance from establishments who wants to reduce their business growth. I question those traditions enact trade barriers against their engagement with Chinese private industries. For me, the inquiry involves the implementation of practical projects whereby knowhow is transferable to Black Chamber organizations for their particular membership groups.

One such way is for small business owners and entrepreneurs to identify a shortage of merchandise in their neighborhood and asked if their local chamber has access to overseas providers. The sensible question can require trade organizations to provide tangible resources based on access to manufacturer and product suppliers from their foreign counterparts. I trust these established overseas counterparts offer face-to-face match making events with specific business interests and guidelines guarantee mutual benefits. My concerns are what happens when any trade organizations are hesitant to release external resources or are unable to provide evidence. I believe members can request how to acquire direct access to foreign manufacturers and suppliers to become part of their educational workshops and seminars. These local trade organizations recognize black entrepreneurs want to serve low to moderate communities. They need a guarantee to acquire those practical skills absent from their local trade organizations.

In America's small communities, there is a need for Black American general merchants to carry a wide selection of goods and where black consumers can go to purchase their items. These merchants can offer a little bit of everything and become small-specialized black retailers who have a whole lot more of one specific thing. Besides, they will differ from other ethnic groups which are the leading shop for the black community rather than a convenient supplement. I believe it's a good strategy for Black-owned wholesalers to form relationships with foreign manufacturers and general merchandise suppliers. They can even become distributors of suitable products and handy device to consumers and retailers in the black community. I imagine when a black person buys an excellent football training aid in a black-owned gas station or corner store because a black wholesaler saw the opportunity and persuades the black store's owners to stock and sell it. There is a significant transport system black America needs to develop to have the distribution of products to support black-owned businesses. With the effects of the global economy on the black business community, I am mindful women truckers will require additional drivers to maintain large-scale development projects. A semi-trailer truck can transport most products sold in black-owned stores from everyday used items to industrial products. Even though transportation is a hard job, black truckers are a crucial component of the Black America supply chain. As black only marketplace changes, there will be a need to increase the number of black millennial truckers. I feel the semi-trailer truck industry is lucrative because the black lady truckers keep the black economy to move forward.

The economic impact of ocean freight and airfreight on international trade is noticeable, just like black economic power impacts on building black wealth. There is no need to avoid foreign trade if you support black-owned businesses. First, some black general store merchants will have to unlearn and relearn how black knowledge does not hinder geographic location. Of course, the reference import and export market strategies for supply chain management, black connections, and black professionals from various business services. These services include procurement, manufacturer freight forwarder, and warehouses. I have a perception; it's a good thing to engage in the global economy. I understand it's a good thing, and the black community can benefit from such involvement. I sense to participate in the worldwide economy simply means we are poised to provide diverse business solutions, and partners that will support black economic growth. Which is to say, "To engage in the global marketplace will illustrate how black marketplace will illustrate how black entrepreneurs are competitive with customer experience, product, and services to worldwide consumers. Our competitiveness inspires forward-thinking decisions and us to engage with neighborhood development projects-- embraces intelligence in the black community. It takes a more resilient black American business supply chain system which is capable to resist sudden shocks and sustain its core function — an essential core to sustains on-time deliveries. I know the answer is not cut and dried. While there will be challenges into what makes a supply chain resilient, there are clear primary reasons for what makes a robust black business owner or black entrepreneurial resistant. The strength directs my focus not only to the problems to support black-owned businesses as a collective but also to practical, achievable, and appropriate solutions to create, maintain, and expand them as well. I know some will argue the influential only pretends to pursue socioeconomic change, while they keep a status quo that benefits them. Black Americans can continue to move in the direction to engage with neighborhood development projects.

I realize how some black-owned businesses lack direct access to foreign markets continue to deprive our community of economic growth. It is in international markets where the absence of Black American trade organizations exist, which can focus on Black small and medium sized enterprises. But, as I have experienced, most trade industry in China will be a great benefit to Black America business owners. Chances are most don't participate in consumer marketplace events in China to seek direct access because they have no foreign representation. In a sense, in 2000 and 2001 on an academic prospect, I may have a false sense of how direct access to Chinese private industries can help me on a personal level. And yet, I understand the importance of an innovative Black America

SME consumer market growth strategy, which focus on mutual sustainable and practical practices within the realm of international trade. I ponder when there are discussions about consumer marketplace in China does Black America want a seat at the table? In a sense it validates the potential role of an trade international trade negotiation team in China for Black America.

To engage in the consumer marketplace, Black American SMEs must understand every product life cycle includes a development phase and a mass production phase. Each stage requires a different skill set. At first glance, behavior to engage in the manufacturing process might be driven by their motivation to act in such a manner. Instead, for others, they source their products from the local wholesaler or retail outlet can be influenced by their behavior. I suppose even though the former or latter assertion is valid or not will depend on how accessible those products are for these black entrepreneurs. In both scenarios, the more direct access these business owners take to engage in the global marketplace, the more they feel it's the right approach to take. The accessible part is another valid reason why Black America small business owners and entrepreneurs need to develop a supply chain network to manage their product life cycle. Most products sell into their neighborhoods from individuals who don't give back to the area. Even though manufacturers of everyday used items operate multiple assembly lines in foreign countries, some entrepreneurs will purchase a handful of these products from non-black wholesalers. Under these circumstances, it can become a common tendency for some wholesalers after additional importation duties to charge a higher cost to these entrepreneurs. Or not. I believe for some black entrepreneurs; there's a hiddencomplexity of direct access to overseas manufacturers. Yet I start to recognize in China certain products are discouraged because of their suggestive improper trade practices. To me, the discouragement of these products is not an attempt to identify the entire industry has improper trade practices. But specific products within an industry are permitted to a handful of merchants and not the whole industry. Particular sectors can provide about thirty or even sixty percent of the total number of products necessary to meet black folk demands.

For some stateside entrepreneurs to understand the concept, they will have to embrace China from an economic equity perspective. Otherwise, the fallout from the lack of acceptance can harm a new creative, collaborative mindset between small and medium sized businesses. To stimulate the mindset, I believe it's sometimes best to visit trade shows and let those ideas come, whereby insights manifest so they might discover their action precedes inspiration. W h e n black entrepreneurs have a certain mindset to build general merchandise stores, develop import and export companies, form supply chain networks, and visit foreign manufacturers, engagement with China is essential within the process. When black individuals sit down each day and discuss their gratitude in the forms of art, music, nature, human kindness, thoughtfulness, and integrity, they become one of the most potent forces on earth. I can only imagine the importance when we take notice of our own epiphany business collaborative insights. We can teach ourselves to have deeper connections with the global market through specific economic development inputs and actions. I seek inspiration in its powerful ways; my confidence grows, which triggers newer insights to higher-level innovative products and services, evoke new ideas and inspiration.

I know we can create incredible businesses no one else has thought of before. I am a visionary with the desire to serve humanity in more significant and more innovative ways. I just imagine how meaningful it will be for Black America to establish a self-sustainable chamber of commerce in China. Then connect it with a measurable amount of micro business enterprises products and services with the greater China region. Of course, once black entrepreneurs start a corporate partnership within the greater China region in vivid detail, they can commence involving both the economic conscious and subconscious mind. They can work to construct foreign trade offices to form business-maps are a compelling necessity to disseminate our social and cultural business opportunities to the world. I write down the decisive universal cooperative partnership with a deep visualization to make it more emotional for me. I understand when the collective engagement in the global marketplace becomes emotional, it won't be economically powerful enough. I need to connect the difference between my global financial identity and partnerships with the development of a new and purpose-driven vision of our global economic future. As I continue to engage in the worldwide economy every single day, I set in motion how I will connect the difference with potential global partners. I need to focus more on whom than how. When I focus on whom, I will allow myself to think much more prominent.

In the same fashion, black entrepreneurs might partner with a one-stop-shop to deliver their product line creation. Before final arrangements are made with the, we can do it all type of business; they will need knowledge about specific challenges which may or may not emerge because of cultural differences. One such problem is they must learn how to manage and handle the extremely fierce competition with third party suppliers in China. To understand the third party process they must improve their knowledge about import and export regulations, local business practices, and supply chain management. Once they acquire the experience, they can grow their competitive advantage even though they may not have a physical presence in China. I trust their competitive advantage will set about to improve once they attain the information to complements the Chinese manufacturer and supplier industry. Black entrepreneurs can discover new ways to achieve greatness when they create their niche competitively and generate trade agreements to benefit their product line. They have access to those same manufacturers and product suppliers from China as non-black wholesalers. At the same time, they have the option to switch away from those non-black wholesalers who import everyday used items from China at factory door prices. For the purpose, let's just say there are various textiles manufactures, electronics providers, and other consumer goods these entrepreneurs lack direct access. As we know, they can go about to benefit from these resources once they start to participate in international business initiatives and learn to resolve our global trade issues. It will be these unpopular hurtful trade barriers for some businesses and consumers. On the other hand, once these economic conscious and subconscious difficulties are aloof, it will become more cost-effective to manufacture and source from China due to black entrepreneurs increase skills and less sufficient trade obstacles.

China dominates global production in industries, from aluminum foil rolls to children's toys to food packaging and processing equipment. Black American business owners will consider cost-effective approaches for engagement with their Chinese counterparts. Some of these procedures will include a change in behavior towards the source of global production will help increase the overall standard of living in the black community. One way to improve the rule is to develop local black wholesalers for better quality products and services. I foresee black consumers will discover why it's worthwhile for these wholesalers to establish new ties with manufacturers and suppliers in China. Once those connections come into fruition, they will not bother to switch back to non-black wholesalers and retailers for their everyday used items. These wholesalers can pick and choose alternative manufacture, and suppliers provide total landed cost for their products. Also, some importers might need to gain outside knowhow to understand their products' landed value. I will assert they can do both. Because if left untouched, it will be more difficult for them to get the total merchandise price once it has arrived at their doorsteps. They cannot obtain the knowledge if they are not part of the process to understand their total landed cost. They can commence seeking the information in such areas as access to original product price, transportation fees (both inland and ocean), customs duty and taxes, tariffs, insurance, and currency conversion, package design, handling, and payment fees. I believe some black entrepreneurs tend not to seek the information because when they manufacture and source their products, they are not be made aware of their total landed cost.

The small black business community must understand the total landed cost since one clever technique for outside companies to deal with extra duties is to pass disproportionate cost increases onto black consumers. The astute practice will be a continuation of unequal economic growth in terms of price inflation targets black communities. I believe the black communities can be hit harder than others by higher fees on certain imports. We need an alternative supply chain network system in order to shift away from unfavorable companies' implementation of higher retail prices into our communities. In such a situation, it's more logical to move towards engagement with the Chinese private industry to understand our product total landed cost. Even so, I believe the challenge to influence others to want to know their product landed cost will be simple. In particular, when there is adequate information about products and services, and Black America lack of engagement in the worldwide market. By and large, it's not merely because the average person does not understand what the landed cost can do to their bottom line. It's because they do not see the benefitsof their own supplychain network.

I recognize it's common for some small business owners, entrepreneurs, and side hustlers to lack precise insights on how to manufacture or source specific products from foreign suppliers. For them, it may seem difficult to recognize what information suppliers need versus what they ask from them. The sort of interaction is troublesome because most suppliers display their stock items will not ask for detailed product specifications. Since the display is their stock item, they can provide immediate service without additional product information. They tend to persuade various small business owners, entrepreneurs, and side hustlers to overlook the fact they are not always right but never wrong when they purchase their stock items. I find when generic product terms are input onto a specific online B2B search engine, it will display a multitude of merchants. The procedure doesn't yield satisfactory results when detail specifications are necessary for any particular product. I think it's not clear about what is the right method to find suppliers since some black entrepreneurs can encounter irrelevant suppliers.

For example, if I need to market a new type of smart device which requires two to three months for material selection, production time, packaging, and transportation. I must provide the manufacturer with enough detailed information about the product design. Within the process, I must verify the manufacturer understands what I want versus what I need. In some situations, until I present many details about my product concept, it's sometimes awkward for online business-to-business (B2B) foreign manufacturers or suppliers to meet my product specifications. The other times, it's easier. I hope to inspire some black American business owners and entrepreneurs to pursue direct face-to-face access to the large-scale marketplace for tangible economic results. For these business-minded individuals, mouth-to-mouth exposure with foreign merchants or   service providers will benefit their particular trade industry. Most industry leaders understand how to utilize online trade-related platforms to grow their products business. There are face-to-face get-togethers behind the scene which yield the first-time collection of global trade-related opportunities for black entrepreneurs to examine. These face-to-face trade-related opportunities promote additional resources with other businesses from different countries and territories.

I believe specific individuals may be able to obtain a better perspective on the latest supply and demand trends for international products and services. While at the same time, various black entrepreneurs can discover how to offer practical merchandise to their local community and global economy. Once they manufacture their custom merchandise to support the black community, they can then understand the importance of product total landed cost on their business. I can never forget the first time many years ago when somebody asked me to get something from China. Although I'm in the middle of trade negotiations, and yet the same question is prevalent today as it was back then. "Can you get me?" It's not too late for black American entrepreneurs to obtain practical experience for engagement with the global economy. Even though China is a great place to start, my knack to gain possible expertise did not end once these trade negotiations finalize. My aptitude continues on a day-to-day basis, even though authentic discussions with entrepreneurs on how to import and export products and services worldwide.

For one thing, entrepreneurs can commence generating innovative workforce development teams in the black community. Collaboration with foreign partners for new international business agreements can be launch with compatible entities enthusiastic about workforce development. In the same fashion, I believe it is necessary to create trade agreements to establish innovative economic projects with foreign partners receptive to improve others' access to the worldwide economy. There is a lesser need for some black entrepreneurs to cling onto the same traditional western methodologies of community development. For these sought out entrepreneurs, their local market has an atmosphere where their knowledge is required when it benefits other communities and not black neighborhoods. The world needs them to obtain direct access so they can collaborate with foreign partners and present new business ideas. Such ideas must be necessary to create a supply chain team through establish trade agreements to benefit the black community. I believe once direct access is proficient, a new level of innovative workforce development will include black individuals.

The benefit of direct access to overseas manufacture and supplier for black entrepreneurs will legitimize exclusion non-black domestic wholesalers' offer higher prices. I believe these international trade criticisms tend to give most entrepreneurs the illusion they cannot conduct direct negotiation with overseas manufacturers for various products. Some local suppliers will say "YES" to their products but cannot guarantee to customize products at fair and reasonable prices. In such situations, I am not sure if the void in service is because they don't have direct access to those types of products or partners. Once the local supplier accepts an initial order, it doesn't guarantee they won't charge a higher price on the second or third customized orders. The next orders may require some local suppliers to charge additional fees because customize procedures may affect their number of shipments, delivery times, and inventory turnover rates. Black entrepreneurs need assistance from overseas organization to acquire direct access with foreign manufacturers and suppliers to eliminate trade barriers. It's a standard practice for entrepreneurs to receive samples from manufacture to approve their product development. Within the process, their specific product can come into fruition because assistance is through a Black America trade organization with relationship to the manufacturer and product suppliers.

9

Remember What They Do

I am sure some individuals will remember just twenty percent of what I say and thirty percent of what I show them; research confirms people will retain up to ninety percent of what they do or replicate. When I inform a group of one hundred Black American SME owners, how to manufacture and source products from Chinese private industries to grow their business; only twenty owners will recall anything. The others will receive some exposure on how to do the procedure; only thirty percent will remember. After the third group of entrepreneurs performs the process, ninety percent of one hundred will learn. I believe black entrepreneurs must do practical projects on how to manufacture and source products from overseas providers. They can discover distinctive trade prospects with foreign colleagues or overseas travel to facilitate trade agreements. While the substantial decline of the U.S. export market in comparison to China between 2000-2019 is evident, there isn't sufficient data on its direct impact on Black American entrepreneurs. The steady constant unspoken predicament is their lack of access to international business forums impacts global trade agreements. Some of these discussions can attribute to equitable job opportunities, better industry collaboration, and smooth supply chain projects for the black community. I recognize unless others have the interest to import products or services with China, ninety percent can learn to get their hands dirty. Just imagine they can generate trade agreements on top of real-world manufacture and product source experiences.

Some black business needs to start with low-risk projects combine local initiatives, community agencies, and other business owners to become proficient in the ability to generate trade agreements. The project is an attempt to identify where developers, individuals, work units, and entrepreneurs can benefit from such development. I think these efforts will have an enormous impact on the reorganization of community development activities, demographic mobility, local and institutional relations with the black community. The overall endeavor can garner substantial resources from those who are somewhat conscious of how foreign trade agreements can benefit low to moderate communities. I foresee a potential opportunity for the greater China region to bestow resources for Black American SMEs to have direct access to manufacturers and product suppliers. Their support can coincide with the development of SMEs will imply they have sustainable such relationships.

I believe it is essential to note black entrepreneurs can take on an active international role and provide quality products for black neighborhoods. They must establish stable overseas relationships to will yield tangible results for the populous black suffering from rundown neighborhood conditions. No accolades through short programs contribute to maintaining weak black areas. I sense bilateral trade agreements between Chinese private industries and Black American entrepreneurs will forge unseen import and export trade cooperation. The focus on bilateral trade agreements will awaken quality of life projects at the forefront of cultural engagement among Black Americans and Chinese people. Several mutual discussions are necessary to spearhead the effort speaks to business development, job creation, industry contract, beautification efforts, and massive property repair ventures. The most prospective advantage is to increase collective projects among stakeholders in the identifiable district and municipal enterprises. I believe such trade agreements can have a considerable impact since each distinct entity will provide sincere efforts to improve the quality of life.

I think a required alternative approach for black business development with distinctive possibilities in the global market. The path I envision will categorize different ranges of commercial entities, and present-day trade barriers minimize growth potential. The operation of a Black Diaspora trade code platform-specific for black entrepreneurs will be necessary to overcome difficulties within the product and trade in the services industry. I imagine the growth of Black American communities with direct access to Chinese manufacturers and product suppliers will develop commerce activities. With the pursuit of local business opportunities and overseas partnerships, resource allocation can improve import and export partnerships. I believe the development of such platforms will replace doubts with new tactical trade solutions to fill in gaps where municipal organizations fall short. I sense it's long overdue for Chinese private industries and Black American entrepreneurs to create new collective partnerships. Through my China experience, I focus on particular trade industries to gain direct access to the global marketplace with tangible economic results. The focus requires practical knowledge so I can decide if it's feasible to pursue specific product or service trade industries to yield a commercial gain. I must understand how to utilize commerce resources to deliver practical merchandise and trade in services to worldwide clients.

The resource can build upon a Black America supply chain network to encompass oversea models, which involve collaboration we need to generate but find hard to access. For example, sport is knowhow. Black Americans learn how to play games through competition against good athletes, not through observation at sports events. One possible way for us to acquire overseas knowhow is to work, study, and live alongside people who already have such knowhow. Within the interconnection, some black individuals' activities need to change from domestic to the global mindset for the development of a supply chain network. I believe it means more brains with high-grade technical and management knowhow need to spend more time outside America to create more opportunities for the black community. The way I perceive it, there is a definite blunder of international commerce opportunities continues to circumvent Black America's economic engagement with other countries and opportunities thereof. I consider the mistake a lack of exposure because other Chinese companies are unaware of the same lack of awareness. Some factories may not see the connection between their resources and those of Black American SMEs to forecast cooperative projects.

There can be some misperception about China lingers within the Black American ideology. The most frequent fallacy is they want to manufacture and source products from China because of low labor costs. I have to remind them I'm not sure which supplier in China they go to, but the truth is China has not been a small labor-cost country for many years. I believe the perception of low-cost labor is not the sole purpose of coming to China from a supply point of view. The sole purpose is because of the skill level, the skill quantity in one Province or City, and the type of required skills essential to generate tangible agreements. One possible underutilize purpose for black Americans is to acquire large-scale experience from travels to and work in foreign countries. The travel commitment needs to happen because its inevitability to our people demand exposure to global resources is transferable to the black community. It's unfortunate some relay on black athletes, entertainers, clergy, and politicians as recognizable for our community to rise and decline in the global society. These individuals are just as responsible as each of us on the economic, cultural, social, and political influence on the upswing or deterioration of black individuals in the international community. I believe some of us will witness pivotal bridge builders foresee a global mindset to stimulates global presence in the pursuit of large-scale global growth. Some recognize the value of products and services companies make and sell in foreign markets estimates in billion of dollars.

The amount of transferrable resources through exposure from one country to a global mindset individual is priceless. I believe a particular consumer market growth percentage is about four times faster than America in the next few years. The Chinese are not a market black entrepreneurs can ignore because it bypasses the U.S. to become the world's largest consumer market. The only conceivable way to understand the market is to acquire awareness about products and trade in services appropriate for consumers. I think it means the formation of a foreign organization facilitates more opportunities for black individuals to gain valuable knowhow, and then so be it. For some black America, small businesses to receive useful resources about specific international conferences and trade events are inclined   to rely on promotion via the overseas chamber of commerce. Some of these symposiums and economic occasions may have, without any intention, overlook influential black community leaders to speak on economic issues for said communities. But what they lack is an outreach program for these individuals to encourage black America to engage in the global market as a commercial gateway. I sense the lack of foresight is because most of these programs do not recruit black businesswomen, businessmen, and startups, which have a large and competitive culture participate within the global economy. Our community does not just have athletes, singers, and dancers, but we cannot demonstrate how particular black individuals are self-sustainable without the involvement of other countries. The type of pro-growth agenda oversight presents opportunities for the black community is so anxious to boost productivity, income, and demand a more reliable connection to the global economy. I fathom some black influencers' can utilize their competitive advantage to retain, create, and expand business owners' comprehensive coverage through various international symposiums and commerce platforms. While others are fictitious to do the same, yet they rely on their means to acquire valuable assets about specific international conferences and trade events for their community.

I read The Negro in Business, by Booker T. Washington and I began to connect those countless businesses to the current day black entrepreneur. As they did then and we continue to do now, to attend black conferences, black expos, black entertainment events, and black sports events. There is an unambiguous difference between industrial revolution advancement then and globalization now. Those business opportunities exist in the hotel boutique, home decor, and office furniture trade industry because they were more accessible to black patrons. In 1907, black America's needs were to engage in innovative domestic industries to redevelop businesses; our present-day problem is we don't have our international supply chain team. I perceive Black American SMEs need a system update to engage with the global economy for door-to-door factory direct products. The system update need acquires an understanding of engagement in foreign trade for their trade-in service expertise.

I discover a need to inform some black entrepreneurs who lack precise awareness about how they will deliver their product specifications. Even though when they correspond with a manufacturer and supplier for their goods, they must understand the importance of how to convey product requirements. Other than how they limit themselves to short message services, screen shots, or third-party download links to illustrate their production concept. For some individuals, the practice, alongside manufacture or product source suppliers, is not without their area of proficiency. I admit they must go beyond The Negro in Business and start to provide information such as the product purpose, product materials, the dimensions, coatings or treatment requirements, free-hand drawings, and compliance standards. And if not, then the present-day Black small business owners and entrepreneurs will continue to receive possible inadequate merchandise not adhere to their product concept. I acknowledge the lack of product concept for some small black-owned businesses, and entrepreneurs can inhibit their direct access to manufactures. One such inhibitor is how they acquire a large number of product concepts and then select a few which shows the most promise. I appreciate those few selection concepts; they will focus on a product benefit the global marketplace.

They can concentrate on product convenience will which save consumers' time and make life easier for them. As well as allow consumers the ability to interfaces with the product for a pleasant and productive experience.

I understand an entrepreneur's focus can be to develop a product non-functional quality such as sturdiness and dependability. Unfortunately, most black entrepreneurs who lack direct access to manufactures can only think about their product concept in terms of a few words. In a practical sense, the stories in The Negro in Business demonstrate successful entrepreneurs are not well known. The book conveys black entrepreneurs with foresight and resourcefulness accomplish success with ethical business codes. I recognize the viewpoints through these businessmen are original thinkers in business. These black entrepreneurs began to provide adequate product specifications with creativity, carefulness, and integrity. Through practical experience, they enhance their competitive merchandise advantage in the overall marketplace. Their possible experience does not specify the percentage of trillion dollars Black Americans buy on an annual basis from import and export products. Within the unspecified portion, some multinational conglomerates develop a supply chain network to allow them to market successful products to the black community. At present, I believe outside knowledge about the black community illustrates what's at stake when particular ethnic groups seem to have our community on lock. Therefore, the Black American trade delegation must meet with their Chinese counterparts to negotiate specific trade agreements to acquire Chinese equipment and supplies to manufacture products. While at these negotiations, they must acknowledge what will be at stake when all develop standard beneficial deals. Again, what's really at stake is a useful practice to establish mutual agreements for a specific product, and brand categories will resonate throughout Black America. Within the sensible method to do more is no overstatement to advocate for the Black America economic growth. Or to dismiss it will lessen our level of engagement in the global economy. Even though these two statements are debatable, I will maintain Black America's economic growth is not a standard occurrence in the global economy. It's time for some black small business owners, entrepreneurs, and side hustlers to expand into the large-scale market - on the worldwide market terms and not on black individuals' time. I observe how some small business owners travel halfway around the world to manufacture and source garments, home products, personal care goods, and tableware for their businesses. To better access equipment and supplies for their products, others utilize various websites or trade negotiators to generate trade agreements. They coexist because specific entrepreneurs have particular knowhow to recognize: whatever creates more trade agreements for them, they will do more of it; and whatever doesn't, they will dismiss it.

The present-day trade practices between Black America and China must lead participants in the global marketplace coalitions. From the position, I learn from my successes and failures while observing others to become significant change agents with Chines private industries. I believe my practical experiences can be the catalyst to initiate changes to build transnational commerce partnerships. I recognize the overall large-scale global economy will be more receptive to bilateral difference makers. The sense of uniformity allows me to appreciate a commonality with other likeminded individuals. A commonality focuses on galvanizes Black SMEs and entrepreneurs who are not solely dependent upon economic growth within America. These thought leaders recognize external economic growth opportunities have their rewards, and they embrace such opportunities. They realize there's a need to connect the difference with other business groups in such areas as products, suppliers, and compliance industries. I know other foreign business organizations must make connections with countries and regions all over the world to strengthen their membership, economic cooperation, and trade. As well as promote their global business influence and world economic impact to make opportunities more receptive to them. Even though to get more engagement from other countries will be tough. I know Black American SMEs can no longer afford to 'stay stagnate,' let alone lose focus on the global marketplace as they witness others find engagement with foreign countries with steady growth. Besides, to be stagnant is long-lived. I feel they can have a steady increase in business engagement, rather than observe trade agreements with other ethnic groups. For a reason, I am concerned Black American SMEs' international economic opportunities will plummet and disappear to where opportunities will no longer exist.

China holds one trillion dollars of treasuries. At the same time, Black America has an annual purchase power of one trillion dollars in America. I concede China exports more to America, and there is a trade imbalance between the two countries. When Black American small business owners travel abroad and witness how others participate in trade shows, they might start to have those uh huh moments. They will commence recognizing how others present global trade distractions in an attempt to dissuade their trade relations with Chinese private industries. Once any particular trade distraction reveals itself, they can seek clarification from the overseas black trade organization. Such organizations are there to make the awareness known within the black community. One-way for some black America small business owners can glance the global marketplace is to associate with overseas black organizations and entrepreneurs to acquire their resources on specific foreign business opportunities. These overseas black organizations and entrepreneurs will provide tangible results built on their direct access with particular country counterparts. The necessary direct access develops through face-to-face negotiations with specific trade guidelines and procedures; it can guarantee mutual benefits. The requirements for black Americans' direct access to the global marketplace is more about strategic linkages between them and the greater China region. I believe Black American SMEs can capitalize on their niche competitive advantage with Chinese private industries. To set in motion, they must possess the definite aptitude to acquire the knowhow to understand the complex business environment, adapt their strategies and business models to the Chinese market, and develop new technologies and services, which cater to the preferences of Chinese consumers. These essential requirements illustrate seven keys below approaches:

1. Must develop a deep (enough) understanding of the Chinese market.
2. Must improve the management of relations with Chinese regulators and the government.
3. They cannot attempt to impose U.S. business models unsuited to the Chinese market.

4. Must learn to handle extreme fierce competition in China.
5. Must acquire the knowhow to manage relations effectively with local business partners.
6. They cannot attempt to impose ideologies developed for the U.S. market on China.
7. Must not have an organizational structure for a slow decision-making process.

I imagine the path forward in China manifestation with profound insight to stimulate a trade organization for Black American SMEs while nurturing their relations with China. In like manner, how to introduce their products and trade in services in cooperation with Chinese private industries to market within the greater China region. I believe its unfortunate Black American SME does not have a corporate directive to form an economic relationship with China to benefit the black community. I know there's a need to be a direct profitable plan to focus on iconic services to enter the Chinese consumer market. Albert Park, an economist at Hong Kong University of Science & Technology, census data from 2000 through 2014, determines compare with other developing countries. China has a more significant proportion of low-end services and sales jobs. At the same time, it lags in professional and technical positions with little information in China about Black Americans' iconic service industries. Their issues and needs tend to underrepresent the chamber of commerce policy and economic discussions. I think Black Americans need specific avenues to provide their quality service throughout the greater China region. Besides, there is a significant disparity in gross revenue for Black-owned businesses as compared to U.S. Hispanic, and Asian-owned firms. The reason is not only a lack of access to capital and resources, but Black American SMEs have to remember what they do to move out of the small-business category into the middle-market category. The middle market is company larger than small businesses, but lower than significant enterprises account for the middle third of the U.S. economy's revenue.

10

Consumption and Innovation

From 2005-2015, Congressional Black Caucus (CBC) member comprised of forty-nine districts of which it estimates those eleven billion dollars of Foreign Direct Investment (FDI) came from Chinese investors. Per the Rhodium Group, a full ninety-eight percent of U.S. congressional districts, four hundred twenty-five out of four hundred thirty-five host Chinese owned companies, which shows increase lobbying power in the United States. In 2016, the Chinese invest forty-eight billion dollars into America. Mergers and acquisitions drive these investments, which indicates Chinese investors continue to use their resources to acquire U.S. assets more than to create new companies. It's terrible to understand the purpose of these investments is to concentrate on fragile communities. Still, instead, they go to projects in more affluent areas like San Francisco, Houston, New Jersey, Chicago, and Baltimore. Even under those dire investment circumstances, in the same year, the Minority Business Development Agency (MBDA) reports there are more than 2.5 million Black-owned businesses in the U. S. generate more than one hundred fifty billion dollars in gross revenue.

Even so, China's 13th Five-Year Plan (2016-2020) focuses on domestic consumption and innovation rather than through massive infrastructure and capacity building investment. The plan estimates to double China's 2010 GDP and per capita income by 2020, to end overcapacity in heavy industry and deal with debt and bad loans. I acknowledge the plan has five development and restructure areas: innovation for quality growth, coordinate across sectors, environment-friendly growth, continue to open abroad and an active role in global governance, and to expand social services. I recognize more details will emerge about the initiative emphasizes the share of the global value chain to raise Chinese made value-added core content in Chinese exports from under twenty percent in 2011 to forty percent by 2020 to seventy percent by 2025. The initiative also pushes private firms to have more strategic say in the standard situation and intellectual property protection, and an increasing amount of Chinese FDI comes from private firms rather than State-Owned Enterprises (SOE). Per the Price Waterhouse Coopers report, Chinese people will spend over ten trillion Yuan ($1.54 trillion) from 2016 to 2020 on senior care, with a one percent increase per year.

The clear indication is Beijing knows where it wants the economy to head. Black American entrepreneurs, through domestic trade organizations, can recognize the growing trend in China. I am concern there's a trend in the U.S. to imply we cannot engage with China. I believe we need a more collective economic strategy with the greater China region because if our businesses continue to lack mutual involvement, then we will stand to lose. And when the black entrepreneur fails, the whole Black community loses access to China's massive infrastructure and capacity building investment. In a sense, the Chinese private industry will provide operational experiences and inroads f o c u s on domestic consumption and innovation in the below sectors:

1. Healthcare – Gerontology, Rehabilitation & Chronic Diseases Care
2. Health and Wellness

3. I.T. – Telemedicine, Mobile Health I.T., Home Health I.T., Facility I.T. solutions, On-Demand Platform, Virtual Reality, Artificial Intelligence, Big Data Analysis, Wearable, Robots, Internet of Things
4. Architectural Design Services
5. Safety Technologies – Emergency Call, Floor Protection
6. Consulting Services & Training

In China, "The service sector plays a much better role to stabilize the overall labor market," says Erna Cui, an analyst at Beijing-based China consulting firm Gavekal Dragonomics. Once Black entrepreneurs focus on the senior care industry in China, it can spur an ever-increase cross border capital flow and integration. The cross border integration can bring them into collaboration with China's health care and high tech private industries for cooperative agreements. The United States Census Bureau says there were 2.6 million Black American-owned firms nationally in 2012, up from 1.9 million or 34.5 percent from 2007. While 9.4 percent of all U.S. firms are Black American-owned in the health care and social assistance sector, the most significant percentage is 19.2 percent. The Atlanta metro area has more Black American-owned firms one hundred seventy-six thousand two hundred forty-five in 2012 than any other metro area besides the New York metro area two hundred fifty-thousand eight hundred ninety. Georgia has more Black American-owned firms in 2012 than any other state two hundred fifty-six thousand eight hundred forty-eight, followed by Florida two hundred fifty-one thousand two hundred sixteen. The District of Columbia, Mississippi, and Georgia were the only states where more than one-quarter of all firms were Black American-owned (34.8 percent, 27.7 percent, and 27.6 percent, respectively).

Among the nation's fifty most populated cities, Black American-owned firms as a percentage of all firms were highest in Detroit and Memphis, Tenn., in 2012 (77.0 percent and 56.2 percent, respectively). "We are encouraged by the overall growth of the minority business community, includes African-American-owned businesses, but we have a lot of work to do, especially to increase gross receipts," said David A. Hinson, National Director at MBDA. "Reaching entrepreneurial parity in size, scope, and capacity is our primary goal." The Congressional Black Caucus (CBC) starts in 1971, and it's great. In 2017, I believed their lack of response to global economic forces harms the black entrepreneurs' opportunity for the Black American community. In particular, I think CBC has no worldwide business and entrepreneurial sector equity strategy between black America and the Chinese private sector. I am curious about Black America's economic empowerment relationship with China. For example, I wonder if an American trade organization signs a two hundred fifty-three billion trade deal with China for American companies, it will not include any Black American small and medium sized enterprises. I believe it's conceivable just like Chinese FDIs; black entrepreneurs will not receive any tangible business opportunities from China. It can be because there isn't a clearinghouse within China for information targets these business owners, and they can fall out of the economic empowerment loop. If so, I believe Chinese organizations see little value in doing direct business with specific black American companies to have no representative office in China.

In 2008, James H. Johnson Jr., Grover C. Burthey III, and Kevin Ghorm wrote an article about Economic Globalization and the Future of Black America. It states, "Throughout history, successful African American entrepreneurs have demonstrated time and again the uncanny ability to turn adversity into opportunity in dealing with internal challenges as well as external threats. African Americans must respond to the current challenges of economic globalization in much the same way: by developing, nurturing, and most important, unleashing the full entrepreneurial potential exists in the African American community". It's my vision to unleash the full entrepreneurial potential will be driven by Black businesses in collaboration with Chinese private industries. To trigger the full potential is to say we need to know about some works of Mao Tse-tung April 16, 1968; A New Storm Against Imperialism can shed some light. Within the article, Chairmen Mao states. "The Afro-American struggle is not only a struggle waged by the exploited and oppressed Black people for freedom and emancipation, but it is also a new clarion call to all the exploited and oppressed people of the United States to fight against the brutal rule of the monopoly capitalist class. On behalf of the Chinese people, I, at this moment, express resolute support for the just struggle of the Black people in the United States". Even at present, it shows Black America has some direct exposure to the Chinese leadership. The type of disclosure is necessary to secure critical information and knowhow from China during the period is up to debate. To date, the lack of direct collaborative pathways for the Black business community in regards to specific products or services agreements with China rests solely on those who have contact with such expertise. The black American society cannot rely upon the traditional American Chamber of Commerce,   and various state economic development office resources in China which do not have their best interest in mind. I now present an opportunity to inform these well-funded, well-respectable black leaders with an economic empowerment plan to support the creation of our Black American Chamber of Commerce in China. Besides, to endorse strategies and tactics to alleviate black America's business lack of access to the global market, country by country, until those countries are accessible.

I deem its necessity to unleash our full potential; direct action needs to provide black entrepreneurs more access to current information for them to stay competitive in the global marketplace. — Dr. Benjamin F. Chavis, Jr., in his article China: New opportunities for African American business states. "I can encourage many of the existing African American Chambers of Commerce in Los Angeles, Houston, Chicago, New York, Georgia, and Florida and other cities across the United States to accelerate their outreach to China." The practice to match Black business owners with mutual opportunities in China to sell goods and services needs to expand. I understand the obligation to create mechanisms will form strategic partnerships with Chinese private industries. Strategic partnerships to provide educational and economic empowerment resources assist black entrepreneurs in meeting those challenges of international trade and commerce.

Some Black entrepreneurs will have to figure out what are their economic empowerment targets with the global economy. I might not have the same objectives others have, but I'm wage confident black entrepreneurs want more worldwide consumers, more engagement, and more sales volume. Black entrepreneurs can expect different types of barriers as they move forward. Some may lack initial capital injection, need to hire local staff, market-entry costs, build bridges between domestic and foreign government officials. They require direct access for manufacture and product source in regards to collaborative economic projects with Chinese private industries. I recognize the creation of an organization in China for economic empowerment sustains black entrepreneurs through entrepreneurship and trade agreements is vital to the development of black communities in America. These collaborative projects among black entrepreneurs and Chinese private industries are essential interaction to connect the difference between cultures.

The collaboration must target mutual expansion projects with China as trade partners to include where both want the other's businesses to be. The partnership ought to include progressive, collaborative markers along the way to target achievements. I foresee mutual expansion developments can be to identify a healthy and successful black entrepreneur are attractive to a Chinese entrepreneur, students, and tourists and creates a loyal customer base. I have a concept appropriate for Black America SME, known as the "Sino-Black Trade Collaborative Business" (SCTCB) initiative. The SCTCB initiative is just what it sounds like -a resource on trade relations with specific targets to connect more black entrepreneurs with Chinese entrepreneurs, students, and tourists who share a similar interest to develop long term economic relationships. The SCTCB initiative will build, connect, and advocate for black entrepreneurs to target more opportunities with Chinese global economic and trade influence. Creativity is vital because it's not common knowledge the "the evil system of colonialism and imperialism arose and throve with the enslavement of Negroes and the trade in Negroes, and it will surely come to its end with the complete emancipation of the Black people," Mao states.

We must target either custom audiences or interest-based audiences because it's not best to leave them to the present or future White House administration. Otherwise, we can waste valuable opportunities to rely on the wrong people. In an article, Black Political Leaders Have Been Elected Across The Country. So What's Next, Bryan Epps states, "We need leaders whose politics are grounded in a radical commitment to Black liberation and will Black leaders not demonstrate such a commitment, we must push them forward or push them out." We ought to expand a China Study Abroad program to enlist young black individuals who have the interest to work, study, and live in China. The particular approach makes sense because it will coincide with our business community needs to have individuals who you engage in everyday life in China. I know there are effective ways to get youth more connections with Chinese entrepreneurs, students, and tourists to acquire long-term business relationships with Black America.

An extensive dialogue between Black America and Chinese private industries has excellent potential to create collaborative commerce opportunities. Within our short-term goals, we must establish an office in China to represents our business community interest. I believe the trade office will be essential to connect the difference among cultures will benefit institutions and organizations need to partake in mutual investment and economic development opportunities. Epps also states, "The Black public's inclination to support or defend Black political leaders had given way to disenchantment seemed to persist up until the present.

Black people appeared to be exhausted by the letdowns—exhausted because sometimes we have exalted Black leaders who will do more harm than good and leap off of their pedestals shortly after their arrival". I believe our long-term goals must create means to bring together stakeholders who have the resources and institutional capacity to support the extensive dialogue between Back America and Chinese private industries. It is through these means the introduction of new technologies can expand economic development opportunities for the global economy. As well as preserve and magnify current stakeholders with regular dialogue among Chinese counterparts to leverage resources, techniques, and expertise on behalf of cross-culture business initiatives. The initiative can influence critical stakeholders to support the establishment of an official trade office in China. The function of the office will be to address critical issues pertinent to the interests of black American entrepreneurs. Chinese engagement will build trust with Black America, who understands global mutual positions to develop collaborative business.

It can probably be said best this way:

"More Collaborate = More Engagement = More Support"

As their business grows, black entrepreneurs engagement with China can grow since there are plenty of additional steps to get more Chinese collaborations. The previous thoughts outline effective ways which can improve black America's economic empowerment through more collaborative opportunities with China. I know to get more engagement with China can be tough. In March 1913, Minton, H. presented a paper entitled,

Early History of Negroes in Business in Philadelphia at the meeting of the American Historical Society. He concludes his formal remarks by stating, "our salvation as a race depends more upon commercial success than upon any other one factor." Given the hostile political environment and racially disparate effects of the POTUS, the writer agrees with Johnson Jr., Burthey III, and Ghorm's evaluation of Dr. Minton's assessment of African American condition in 1913 holds equal, if not more significant, weight today. We must be diligent in supporting and creating resources for a trade office in China which targets black economic empowerment. The effort is the best way to ensure black entrepreneurs to focus on domestic consumption and innovation exposure to global trade opportunities through China. I am hopeful the simple yet effective approach can help provide some guidance.

11

Forward Path

I know my path forward is to unlearn nonproductive business practices and then relearn how to shift into a cultural and economic alignment with the Chinese private industry. These unlearn and relearn approaches do not facilitate alterations of bias in public laws and regulations practices stagnate such opportunities. For me, it is to circumvent an indifferent system obscures access to foreign business partnerships for the benefit of the black community. One systematic structure is to provide practical knowledge for black entrepreneurs to enable a connection between them and international entities. I no longer ponder how to form transcontinental business relationships, surpass these barriers for any particular industry. The relationship involves direct access to known products and services connect the difference to enhance global joint opportunities. My concept for global business integration means: "The principal criterion for Black businesses or population is to collect and cultivate a business relationship with Chinese private industries."

My perspective in American urban business opportunities my differ from other individuals in particular when non-urban communities engage in different business pursuits. The first and fundamental difference between blacks and other ethnic groups and specific urban communities is access to overseas suppliers. Without immediate attention, I imagine the lack of useful skills for some urban blacks to engage in foreign markets can be a severe challenge from potential growth prospects. Unlike most non-urban businesses, it's feasible they tend to receive more pragmatic business opportunities through state and local economic development organizations. I feel they must launch strategic partnerships within China to enables commerce chances for the Black community. Such commerce prospects provide specific global access and streamline current business opportunities as they occur. I believe Black America will benefit from a simple unlearn and relearn upgrade about Chinese private industries to substantial core universal commercial endeavors. Our shift in mindset will improve access to commercial, community, and educational resources with foreign trade offices.

I value black business needs exposure to products and services projects from overseas advocates for collaborative commerce projects with a like-minded acquaintance. Even though some facilitators may include primary, secondary, and tertiary centers of trade, they provide various aspects of business development. I think with the level of several trade centers to manufacture and possible collaborative projects, the black business will be given chances to expand into other areas. With the potential expansion, I anticipate global access for businesses will decrease economic disparity among neighborhoods and local regions. Black companies can adopt a large-scale collective approach due to struggle against their competitors, in particular, access to different products and services. I notice how some businesses tend to focus on merchandise reflects cultural and economic differences and not occupation and industry transformation for particular neighborhoods. The emphasis continues to remain a nuisance in high-unemployed areas separate black businesses and residents from each other. Even though individual companies are under attack, they have a series of built-up properties of various sizes and degrees. I believe when they separate themselves from other black-owned businesses, residential segregation occurs based on occupations. In such a situation, the black enterprise can utilize Chinese private industries for manufacture and source products to maximize job creation in their community. The process will create a career and trade makeover will not separate business from the people. It will build on the knowhow links black communities to innovative ideas to reflect their cultural and economic difference.

I understand some black businesses lack direct access to merchandise due to insufficient commerce modules to favor traditional methods over practical project techniques. For example, in some neighborhoods, business growth is a pawn to globalization alongside cultural-economic conditions subverts economic development projects. I perceive there are bias individuals within local municipalities who utilize traditional methods to suppress opportunities from the black community. They are plausible to disorganize economic development projects. I believe such patterns are possible diversion deters black entrepreneurs from establishing their supply chain network with Chinese manufacture and product suppliers to generate trade agreements and improve the betterment of their community. Our path forward can expose the necessity for Black American SMEs' global business concept to maintain the level of wealth and comfort more suitable to economic equity.

Some entrepreneurs may not understand how the procedure requires a possible departure from their present model to enhance business growth. Unlike what underlines the lack of access, I recognize the approach contributes to Black American SMEs' ascension for business development. I believe in expanding their business model is essential rather than spontaneous and creative. Within the expansion process, some may have confusion about how to do international business development. Some may have opinions their efforts are not suitable for the greater China region. They must realize, as I do, through the use of technological advance resources, the mindset can prohibit their business growth. I understand, accessing Chinese manufacturers and product suppliers involves specific practical skills. Requires the implementation of thoughtful projects that increases their desire to generate partnershipagreements with the Chinese private industry.

I believe a reorganization of black business development strategies can shed a great deal of light on the roles of blacks who study, live, and work in China can benefit Black American SMEs in the United States. The basic necessity is the establishment of a business association in China which has access to Chinese private industries to partner with black-owned businesses. I think there is a need to engage some municipal to provide resources to support black-owned companies. When a black business association adopts international integrity as a code of conduct against systematic racist practices, there will be a sense of achievement for urban or rural black business owners. The business association is necessary since strategic partnership demonstrates how involvement between Black American SME and Chinese private industries is necessary for the global economy. Whether the business association is for the good or worse, the approach is a an appropriate insight into black business development. I believe our path forward intertwines with the Black American SMEs' economic survival even before marketable instinct demands an adaptation to the globaleconomy.

I am optimistic the current possibility of a Black America trade agenda with the greater China region, also known as the second leading economy, seems like something can happen within the next ten years. I know it's real when Black American SMEs have a direct connection to Chinese manufacture and product supplier, who has not been their resource; it cannot be challenging to bring into existence. It can be easy to overlook just what a big deal it is. The economic equity potential is about to get much more real for Black American SMEs across America now China industry has become the primary global manufacturer and product supplier. I believe for SME to miss the next ten-year opportunity, as a direct result of the previous twenty will be disastrous. In some instances, I think most SMEs believe their expectation to engage with China both in terms of the supply and trade in service seems out of reach. I know all opportunities in both have not closed in industries perform inner-city revitalization projects, an essential source for job creations for Black America.

To my astonishment, there hasn't been any previous momentum in 2000 to establish a Black America trade organization in China. Not only will Black American SMEs engage in partnership with the greater China region. I predict an increase in trade show participation in China is due to a motivated interest from Black America small business owners. The most important motivation for black entrepreneurs' expansion with the Chinese private industry is the need for economic equity in America. These entrepreneurs ought to develop partnerships to make up for the lost time. I think cooperation with Chines private industry will come just as Black American SME prepares to implement their initial cost-efficient urban renewal projects. It will probably be worth to mention even if I haven't partaken in those China Study Abroad programs in 2000 and 2001, my experience with the world's largest manufacturer and product supplier will have been mute. I am also mindful there's a good chance my knowhow will have been absent about its economic impact on the global economy. While the country continues its Open Door Policy, some suppliers' productivity is more sustainable than others. It can mean partial access to Chinese private manufacture and product suppliers. Or it might say I will have had a harder time understanding the import and export industry, like most Black American SMEs, have been wanting to understand. I believe Black America has passed the point where we can no longer ignore China's commerce events. And--if SMEs haven't already-- it's probably time to make plans for full engagement with the greater China region to secure Black America's economic growth. It isn't hard to see why I perceive black entrepreneurs can challenge the status quo on Black America's financial plan and establish a supply chain network with the Chinese private industry. At least for me its starts with freeze cups.

CHINA TRADE SHOWS PARTICIPATION

1. Bicycle & E-Bike Exhibition
2. China Import and Export Fair (Canton Fair)
3. China Chamber of Commerce for Import and Export of Machinery and Electronic Products (CCCME)
4. China Adult Care Expo
5. China Beauty Expo (CBE)
6. China Children, Baby and Maternity Expo (CBME)
7. China Cross-Border eCommerce
8. China Daily-Use Articles Trade Fair
9. China International Import Expo (CIIE)
10. China Medical Equip Fair (CMEF)
11. China Toy Expo
12. ChinaPlas
13. China International Organic Green Food & Ingredients Exhibition (CIHIE)
14. Cosmoprof Asia
15. East China Fair
16. GSMA WMC Shanghai
17. Guangzhou International Nutrition &Health Food and Organic Products Expo
18. Healthplex & Nutraceutical China
19. Hotel Plus
20. Kitchen & Bath China
21. Lifestyle Show Shanghai
22. Natural & Organic Products Asia
23. Ordos Cashmere Trade Show
24. ProPak China
25. Shanghai International Coffee Industry Expo
26. Shanghai Private Label Fair

27. Week for International Environmental Technologies China (WieTec)
28. Wenzhou Leather & Shoes Material
29. Yiwu Cultural Products Trade Fair
30. Yiwu International Commodities Fair
31. Zhengzhou Feifan Exhibition

INDEX

A

Adversity into opportunity, 131

African American, 130-132, 136

Afro-American, 131

B

Black America foreign trade office, 14-15, 85

Black America small business, 52, 65, 103, 117, 123, 141

Black American small and medium sized Enterprise (SME), 13, 130

Black Political Leaders Have Been Elected, 134

Black American youth, 63

Bowen, Olufunke Dr., 25-26, 29

Brick-and-mortar stores, 64

Brown, Carlton J. Dr., 26, 29, 65

Buy Black campaigns, 7, 70

C

Capital Normal University (CNU), 26-27, 29, 31

Chamber organizations, 74, 85, 99

Chavis, Benjamin F. Dr., 132

China court system, 29

China Study Abroad Program, 21, 24-26, 29, 31, 134-135,151,

Chinese Benevolent, 32

Chinese media, 75

Chinese Professional Club in Savannah, 32

Chinese youth, 79

Classroom modules, 57-58, 61-62, 70

O

Open Door Policy, 28, 74 80, 81, 142
Opportunities in China's Senior Care Market, 128-129

P

PAN Haixiao Professor, 51
Phil Morrison Trio featuring Keith Williams, 43
Product life cycle, 103
Product source, 4-6, 13-14, 64, 66-67, 83-84, 92, 94, 113, 119, 133
Prominent black voices, 65
Purpose of disturbance, 61

R

Rhetorical Narratives of Black Entrepreneurs, 65

S

Savannah State University (SSU), 21, 23-27, 29, 31-33
Severe Acute Respiratory Syndrome (SARS), 48-49
Shanghai American Chamber of Commerce, 37
Shanghai South Railway Station, 44
Shanghai Teachers University (STU), 27, 29
Shanghainese, 13
Shift in global economic influence, 6
Silver, Joseph H. Sr. Dr., 25-26, 29
Sino-Black Trade Collaborative Project (SBTCP), 133
Smart Toys Market 2019-2024, 22, 48, 54, 93, 106
Standard of living in the black community, 107
Stop and Stare, 40

AUTHOR'S BIOGRAPHY

William D. Frazier is the Co-Founder and Global Business Developer of Shanghai-America Direct Import & Export Co. Ltd. and author of Black American Entrepreneur in China: Connecting Industry and Cultural Differences.

A professionally trained global business developer, William has spent the two decades as a reliable international "on the ground" product and service in trade coordinator for business units, product lines, and China import and export operations.

Shanghai, China-based entrepreneur, William D. Frazier writes books, on the sustainability of a product and trade-in service import and export company to generate trade agreements with China private industries. He's best known to have strong strategic acumen to implement different trade deals across the greater China region. He's also a trusted advisor who represents company centralized complex supply chain projects with multiple industries. He enjoys collaborative projects with clients to identify and eliminate trade conflicts, cultivate, and mentor procurement teams for small to medium value projects. William loves to give lectures on China Study Abroad program and Chinese private industries' collaborative prospects with small and medium-size enterprises. He's an avid outdoorsman who appreciates open water diving, salsa dancing, and hiking and camping with family and friends. He currently resides in Shanghai, China with his wife Peng Rui.

CPSIA information can be obtained
at www.ICGtesting.com
Printed in the USA
LVHW010032300620
659354LV00020B/2466